Rappaccini's Daughter

IN THE CLASSROOM

ALSO BY SHARON ADELMAN REYES

Engage the Creative Arts:
A Framework for Sheltering and Scaffolding
Instruction for English Language Learners

The Trouble with SIOP®:
How a Behaviorist Framework, Flawed Research, and
Clever Marketing Have Come to Define – and Diminish –
Sheltered Instruction for English Language Learners
(with James Crawford)

La Palabra Justa:
An English-Spanish/Español-Inglés Glossary of
Academic Vocabulary for Bilingual Teaching and Learning
(with Salvador Gabaldón and José Severo Morejón)

Diary of a Bilingual School:
How a Constructivist Curriculum, a Multicultural Perspective, and a
Commitment to Dual Immersion Education Combined to Foster Fluent
Bilingualism in Spanish- and English-Speaking Children
(with James Crawford)

Teaching in Two Languages:
A Guide for K–12 Bilingual Educators
(with Tatyana Kleyn)

Constructivist Strategies for
Teaching English Language Learners
(with Trina Lynn Vallone)

Rappaccini's Daughter
In the Classroom

Readers Theater Adaptations and Other
Creative Activities for Teaching the Classic Story
by Nathaniel Hawthorne

SHARON ADELMAN REYES

# DiversityLearningK12
PORTLAND, OREGON

Copyright © 2016 by DiversityLearningK12 LLC
All Rights Reserved

The publisher grants individual teachers who have purchased this book (or for whom it has been purchased) permission to reprint "reproducibles" provided in Part III. But reproduction for an entire school or school district, or for any commerical purpose, is prohibited without the express written permission of the publisher. No other parts of this book may be reproduced or transmitted in any form, electronic or mechanical—including photocopying, recording, course readers, electronic reserves, posting on the Internet or other online media, or any information storage and retrieval system—again, without the written permission of the publisher.

For inquiries about permission to reprint, send email to:
info@diversitylearningk12.com

Or send postal mail to:
DiversityLearningK12
P. O. Box 19790
Portland, OR 97280

ISBN 978-0-9847317-5-6

Library of Congress Control Number: 2016908289

Library of Congress Subject Headings:
1. Young Adult Drama, American.
2. Fiction—Adaptations.
3. Hawthorne, Nathaniel, 1804–1864.

Book design and typography by James Crawford
Cover illustration compliments of Hawthorne in Salem
Printed in the United States of America
First edition
10 9 8 7 6 5 4 3 2 1

*In memory of my grandmother,
Florence Berg Adelman*

Contents

PREFACE ix

INTRODUCTION
Who is Rappaccini's Daughter? 1
   How to Use "Rappaccini's Daughter" in the Classroom 2

PART I
Strategies 5

  Dramatic Arts
    Readers Theater 6
    Greek Chorus 7
    Improvisation 10
    Theatrical Production 11
    Aromas to Evoke Mood 12

  Creative Writing
    Calligraphy 14
    Acrostic Poems 15
    Structured Poetry 16
    Script and Story Writing 19

  Visual Art
    Instant Accordion Books 20
    Character Mind Maps 22
    Character Self-Portraits 24

  Movement and Music
    Jazz Chants 25
    Rap 27

PART II
Teacher Resources 29

  Readers Theater
    Production Notes 30
    Follow-Up Activities 31
    Strategy Progressions 32

Historical and Literary Background
- Nathaniel Hawthorne and Tomaso Albinoni 36
- Origins of "Rappaccini's Daughter" 37
- Adaptations of Hawthorne's Story 38

Reference Materials
- Dramatic Arts 40
- Readers Theater 40
- Aromas to Evoke Mood 40
- Greek Chorus 40
- Jazz Chants 40
- Book Arts 41
- Accordion Books 41
- Calligraphy 41
- Fine Arts in Spanish 41
- Creative Arts Activities for English Language Learners 41
- Hawthorne 41

PART III
Reproducibles 43

"Rappaccini's Daughter"
- Story Synopsis 44
- Original Story by Nathaniel Hawthorne 45

Scripts
- Readers Theater, Secondary Level 67
- Readers Theater with Greek Chorus, Secondary Level 83
- Readers Theater, Middle School Level 101
- Readers Theater with Greek Chorus, Basic Level 115
- Theater, Secondary Level 131
- Theater, Secondary Level (Booklet Format) 145

Handouts
- Accordion Book Template 155
- Accordion Book Template with Poetry 159
- Jazz Chant 163
- How to Write a Rap 167
- "Rappaccini's Rap" 175
- Exploring "Rappaccini's Rap" (Teacher Reference) 179
- "Rappaccini's Rap" Answer Key 180

Acknowledgments 183

Preface

WHAT WOULD YOU DO *if you fell in love and then discovered that the person you had fallen in love with was poisonous? Not figuratively poisonous, but literally poisonous?*

My audience, made up of middle and secondary educators, was immediately attentive, yet no one spoke up. Clearly, they had not expected a professional development session to begin in this manner. I pressed on.

Really, what would you do?

"Look for a cure?" came the first tentative response.

"Leave fast!"

"I married him!"

"It wouldn't matter to me because nothing is more important than love."

The question to which attendees responded is fundamental to the story of "Rappaccini's Daughter," by Nathaniel Hawthorne. It is an intriguing one for adults to consider, but it is especially evocative for adolescents. The two central characters in this story are young and romantically involved. And they are simultaneously caught up in a moral dilemma. This makes "Rappaccini's Daughter" an ideal choice for secondary school students, who can usually identify with both of these predicaments.

But theme is not the only ingredient necessary to catch and hold our attention—the attention that precedes literary engagement. Emotional response is powerful because it is so central to our existence as human beings. Because arts-based activities tap our emotions, they provide ideal opportunities for integrating passion with intellect, for exploring the meaning that characters attach to their actions—in short, for understanding and appreciating literature.

The activities in this book draw from a wide range of art forms to bring the story of "Rappaccini's Daughter" to classroom life. From Readers Theater to Structured Poetry, from Character Mind Maps to Rap, teachers will find numerous strategies that they can use to engage their students in a study of "Rappaccini's Daughter." Included are teaching resources filled with ideas for instruction, as well as reproducibles for immediate use in both secondary and middle-school classrooms.

My hope is that these activities will also serve as a springboard for imagining and designing creative activities for other literary works covered in the English and Language Arts curricula. Copyright restrictions generally do not prevent teachers from using or adapting short story excerpts from contemporary literature (known as "fair use") for educational, noncommercial purposes in their classrooms. When in doubt, simply write to the publisher and ask permission. For using or adapting a full work, however, U.S. copyright law now protects literary rights for the life of the author plus 75 years. Thus, commercially published scripts for Readers Theater, such as those featured in this book, are usually adapted from classic literature in the public domain. Also bear in mind that anything originally published before 1923 is no longer under copyright and may be reproduced freely.

Examples of stories from classic literature that could be used to create Reader's Theater scripts include *A Christmas Carol,* by Charles Dickens; "The Dead," by James Joyce; and "The Blue Hotel," by Stephen Crane. In addition to their literary merit, these stories share other attributes that make them suitable for Readers Theater adaptation. Each of them has multiple characters, a good balance of narrative and dialogue, and a relevant theme. The dialect in "The Blue Hotel" can be easily understood or adapted to standard English, and although the characters are predominantly male, their roles can be performed by either boys or girls.

All of these stories (and many more) are easily available on the Internet through Google and other search engines. While some may be lengthy, students can be involved in script adaptation, encouraging them to think deeply about the reading material.

To have students compose Jazz Chants, Character Mind Maps, or other creative works based on literature, no permissions are necessary. In fact, teachers have been engaging students in such activities for many years. This book simply provides a framework for doing what outstanding educators have always strived for—to make learning exciting and to turn the classroom into a place where students want to be.

Rappaccini's Daughter

in the classroom

INTRODUCTION
Who is Rappaccini's Daughter?

HER NAME IS BEATRICE—Beatrice Rappaccini. She is the lovely and mysterious daughter of Doctor Giacomo Rappaccini, a scientist, botanist, and medical researcher.

Doctor Rappaccini cultivates a garden of poisonous plants in his wondrous and exotic garden. Beatrice has been brought up to care for them. In the process, she has become resistant to their poisons, but also poisonous to others.

The narrative from which Hawthorne probably drew this story can be traced back to a traditional folktale from India. It involves a beautiful girl who has been transformed into a kind of living poison and used as a weapon of political revenge. Hawthorne's version is set in Renaissance Italy. A young man, Giovanni Guasconti, has just relocated to attend the University of Padua. He happens to rent a room overlooking Doctor Rappaccini's lush, locked garden. From this vantage point, Giovanni is able to view the stunning Beatrice, confined within as she tends her father's plants. He is enticed by a housekeeper who unlocks the gate for a small bribe, giving him entrance to the garden. There he meets and falls in love with the extraordinary Beatrice.

Giovanni eventually notices Beatrice's troubling effect on the plants in the garden. He sees fresh flowers wither and insects die when exposed to her breath. Giovanni's mentor, Professor Pietro Baglioni, warns him that Doctor Rappaccini is not to be trusted. But, having fallen in love with Beatrice, Giovanni ignores the professor's advice.

Soon Giovanni begins to notice the consequences of his association with Beatrice. He must admit that she is poisonous and that he is becoming poisonous as well. In the meantime, Baglioni gives Giovanni a small vial, explaining that it contains the antidote for Beatrice's poison.

Giovanni confronts Beatrice with his new knowledge of her nature. She urges him to look past her poisonous exterior to see her pure and innocent essence. Giovanni produces the vial filled with the antidote, believing that, by sharing it with Beatrice, they will be able to stay together. She grabs the vial in order to check its safety by drinking it first. But, as poison has been her life, the only antidote is death. Beatrice dies in the garden as Doctor Rappaccini looks on.

How to Use "Rappaccini's Daughter" in the Classroom

If you are a Language Arts or English teacher, you have probably taught literary works before. You don't need to throw away the techniques you have found successful in order to use the activities described in this book. Rather, this is a collection of learning strategies that are meant to augment and enrich your lessons. Use whichever ones best suit your purposes, keeping in mind your students' interests and your own teaching strengths. For example, supplement a discussion of the characters by creating Structured Poems about their feelings toward each other. Or employ multiple strategies in an exciting progression toward that end, using the suggested activity sequence or inventing your own. One option would be to begin with a Reader's Theater production and end with "Rappaccini's Rap."

This book is organized in three parts: Strategies, Teaching Resources, and Reproducibles. All are based on the Hawthorne story.

The teaching strategies that are applied to "Rappaccini's Daughter" are arts-based, incorporating aspects of drama, creative writing, music, movement, and visual art. Because they touch our emotions, they can have instant appeal and promote student engagement.

The teacher resources include detailed directions on using the strategies with your students, historical and literary background information, and resources to consult if you are inclined to dig deeper into using specific arts-based strategies.

Reproducibles are included to facilitate immediate use of these strategies. For example, you can choose from among the four Readers Theater scripts the one that is most appropriate to your students. Or you can distribute the Rap handouts to guide your students in creating their own "Rappaccini Rap." For convenience, Hawthorne's original story is included as well.

The number of students who are in the process of learning English as an additional language is increasing. Many of the teaching strategies in this book, Jazz Chants and the use of a Greek Chorus, for example, provide the motivational context and communicative framework in which English can be acquired. Some of the reproducibles, as exemplified by the basic level Readers Theater script, are particularly suited for English learners. Teachers who want to locate more resources for teaching their ESL students can find them in the resource section.

Start where you are most comfortable. Watch what happens. Improvise a bit along the way. See where student interest leads. Explore together. And have fun.

Part I
Strategies

Dramatic Arts
Readers Theater
Greek Chorus
Improvisation
Theatrical Production
Aromas to Evoke Mood

Creative Writing
Calligraphy
Acrostic Poems
Structured Poetry
Script and Story Writing

Visual Art
Instant Accordion Books
Character Mind Maps
Character Self-Portraits

Movement and Music
Jazz Chants
Rap

Readers Theater

Goal: To appreciate literature

Readers Theater is the oral interpretation of literature adapted for a scripted performance. It is a minimalist production that is meant to highlight the original author's voice by keeping the audience focused on the printed word. For this reason scripts are not memorized, but read aloud by the performers. Nor is the action elaborately staged or choreographed; it is acted out symbolically through gesture and facial expression.

Readers Theater provides access to understanding literature in multiple ways. Because it emphasizes dialogue, the present tense is used extensively. Dramatic reading allows for modification of speech through pacing and intonation, as well as gesture and facial expression. Small, symbolic props and costume pieces provide visual and manipulative aids to understanding. As students prepare for performance, they engage in multiple practice sessions, allowing them to develop different perspectives with each repetition.

Materials

Scripts
Symbolic props and costumes
Essential oil spray (optional; *see page 12*)
Musical selection and audio equipment (optional)
PowerPoint background slides (optional)

Guidelines

Blocking, costumes, and props are minimal. Stage sets, if used at all, are simple and symbolic. Characters are typically seated, usually in a pattern that highlights their relationships to each other. The performance may feature either a single narrator or multiple narrative voices. The script should not be memorized, but kept visible to emphasize the written word. Students should be familiar enough with it to read expressively and to occasionally avert their eyes from the page.

When using the arts for educational purposes, the emphasis should be on the creative process, not the performance. If priority is placed on impressing the audience, superficiality can be the result, with the students "playing at" rather than becoming the characters. Focusing on meaning, by contrast, fosters a deeper understanding of the characters and the dramatic situations in which they find themselves.

Greek Chorus

Goal: To understand the role of the Greek Chorus in Greek drama; to guide understanding of and provide focus to the text

The Greek Chorus was a homogenous group of performers in the plays of classical Greece. Chorus members provided commentary with a single collective voice on the dramatic action occurring before them. They were similarly costumed and positioned, either at the edge of the stage or in the orchestra pit, for the duration of the performance. For adaptation to Readers Theater in the classroom, the positioning of the Greek Chorus in the performance area may be reconsidered.

The chorus was a central feature of Greek drama. Its role was not only to observe and comment, but also to add a sense of spectacle, to help the audience follow the performance, to provide time for scene changes, and to give the main actors a break. In ancient Greek theater, the chorus often expressed what the lead actors could not say—their hidden fears, doubts, and secrets. It also provided characters with insight and moral guidance. The idea behind this strategy is to adapt the Greek Chorus to a literary work with moral and ethical dimensions.

Four different Readers Theater scripts for "Rappaccini's Daughter" are provided in this volume *(see pages 67–129)*; two contain a Greek Chorus and two do not. Giving students an opportunity to write their own lines for a Greek Chorus can engage them in discussing themes, character motives, and literary elements such as foreshadowing.

Materials

Scripts (lines may also be memorized)
Identical robes or fabric coverings for each chorus member (optional)

8 RAPPACCINI IN THE CLASSROOM

Guidelines

The lines of the Greek Chorus may be developed by the teacher, the students, or everyone collectively. As illustrated by the following examples, the Greek Chorus can serve a variety of functions in dramatic productions.

Observe and comment on the dramatic action

NARRATOR ONE: Giovanni awoke the next morning to a burning and tingling pain in his right hand. This was the same hand that Beatrice had held in her own when he was about to pluck one of the purple flowers. On the back of that hand there was a purple print of four small fingers, and on his wrist there was a purple print of a thumb. But Giovanni was so love-struck that he wrapped a handkerchief around his hand and wondered what had stung him. Soon he forgot his pain while thinking about Beatrice.

GREEK CHORUS: Love, aaaaahh, love!

NARRATOR TWO: After the first meeting with Beatrice, there was a second, a third, and a fourth, until meeting Beatrice in the garden was what he lived for. Beatrice felt the same way about Giovanni. And yet they had not kissed, nor held hands, nor even touched but once.

GREEK CHORUS: Love, aaaaahh, love!

Find opportunities to foreshadow

NARRATOR ONE: A long time ago, a young man named Giovanni Guasconti came from Naples, in the south of Italy, to study at the University of Padua. Giovanni did not have much money. He could only afford to rent one room in an old house. In the past, the house had been the palace of a nobleman. This nobleman had met a tragic fate.

GREEK CHORUS: Tragic fate, tragic fate.

NARRATOR ONE: And that gave Giovanni a strange sense of worry.

GREEK CHORUS: Fate, fate, fate, fate.

DRAMATIC ARTS 9

Issue warnings

GIOVANNI: Dearest Beatrice, all is not lost. Look! Here is a medicine a wise doctor gave me. It is made from herbs that are the opposite of your father's poison. Let us drink it together and we will be cured.

GREEK CHORUS [softly]: Don't drink it! Don't drink it!

BEATRICE: Give it to me! I will drink it first. You must wait to see what happens to me before you drink it.

GREEK CHORUS [louder and more insistent]: Don't drink it! Don't drink it!

Reflect characters' unresolved dilemmas, hidden fears, doubts, secrets

GIOVANNI: Am I awake? Have I lost my senses? What is this being? Beautiful? Or terrible?

GREEK CHORUS: Beautiful or terrible? Terrible or beautiful?

NARRATOR THREE: A butterfly seemed to be attracted by Beatrice and it fluttered above her head. Beatrice looked up and it fell at her feet, dead. Did the insect die from her breath? Maybe Giovanni had imagined it. Again Beatrice crossed herself sadly.

GREEK CHORUS: Terrible or beautiful? Beautiful or terrible?

Raise ethical concerns, provide insight or moral guidance, highlight themes

NARRATOR ONE: Just at that moment, Baglioni looked out from the window and called out loudly, in a tone of triumph mixed with horror.

BAGLIONI: Rappaccini! Rappaccini! And is this the result of your experiment?

GREEK CHORUS: Is this worthy of science? Is this worthy ... worthy ... worthy ... worthy ...

[fade to silence]

Improvisation

Goal: To develop empathy and understanding of human behavior through identification with literary characters

Improvisation (a.k.a. "improv") is the impromptu enactment of scenarios with endings that may or may not be previously determined. For example, using their own words and, if possible, costume pieces and props from the Readers Theater production, students dramatize characters and situations from "Rappaccini's Daughter." Here are some possible scenarios:

- *Lisabetta enticing Giovanni into Rappaccini's garden*
- *Giovanni's first meeting with Beatrice in the garden*
- *Giovanni and Baglioni's chance meeting in Padua*
- *Baglioni warning Giovanni of Beatrice's poisonous nature*

Another option is to improvise scenes that might have occurred, but were not part of Hawthorne's story. The endings can be predetermined or open-ended. For example:

- *Rappaccini talking to Beatrice about various tasks in the garden*
- *One of Giovanni's numerous visits with Beatrice in the garden*
- *Rappaccini's interaction with Giovanni immediately after Beatrice dies*
- *Lisabetta telling Giovanni that he must move because he is now poisonous*
- *Giovanni seeking help for his now-poisonous condition from Baglioni*

Successful improvs can be written down by students, added to the Readers Theater script, and staged as an extension of the original story. Or an entire production of "Rappaccini's Daughter" could be created through improvisation, practicing scenes one at a time.

Materials
Costume pieces and props (optional)
Paper and pen for script writing (optional)

Guidelines
Try to keep the scenarios as simple as possible to retain focus. Remember that authenticity is the key. Students should not be overacting scenes or stereotyping characters, but should strive for natural, believable reactions to each situation.

Theatrical Production

Goal: To enhance the appreciation of literature

Staging a theatrical production can be an exciting venture for students of all ages, but it does bring challenges. For example, students may become competitive over favored roles, and there may not be enough roles of any kind for all who are interested. One solution is double casting, which gives more students an opportunity to perform and also provides "understudies" in case of an actor's illness or absence. (It would be wise to have two performances if the play is double cast.) Adding a tech crew and other production roles can also create opportunities for more student involvement.

A common pitfall of memorized plays is that dialogue can be stilted. This happens when students perform caricatures, rather than dramatizing how a character thinks and feels. Many of the strategies in this book have been designed to illuminate the inner life of the characters, ultimately helping students to portray them authentically. Thus, studying "Rappaccini's Daughter" through cognitively and emotionally engaging activities can help students create more authentic portrayals of the characters on stage.

All of this is a time-consuming process, much more so than rehearsals for a Readers Theater production. Yet it would be a shame to discourage students who are enthusiastic about the Hawthorne story. An alternative to using classroom time would be to produce "Rappaccini's Daughter" as an after-school activity. A theater script and staging directions begin on page 131.

Materials
Costumes, props, and set pieces; backdrops (optional)

Guidelines
Staging a production will require a director to block the play and guide the actors. Other roles, such as costume director, stage manager, and set designer may be helpful in distributing responsibilities. All of these can be filled by students, with adult guidance. If the teacher is unable to participate, an interested parent (or parents) might be recruited to do so.

Aromas to Evoke Mood

Goal: To enhance motivation for learning activities by creating an evocative atmosphere

Aromatherapy involves the use of extracted, highly concentrated oils from materials such as woods, nuts, seeds, resins, herbs, trees, and flowers. The scents of these essential oils act upon the limbic system, the structures of our brain that stimulate emotion and long-term memory. The olfactory effects can be intense, impacting mood by creating and renewing feelings associated with particular scents. Thus, aroma can enhance the evocative possibilities in Readers Theater productions. An aromatherapy recipe suggestive of the fragrance of Rappaccini's garden and Beatrice's breath is provided below. It can be sprayed in the air between appropriate scene breaks, when the lights are dimmed.

Materials

Essential oils
Water
Spray bottle

Guidelines

Essential oils should be mixed only by the teacher. For maximum effect, spray the scents into the air when the students are not in the room or when the lights are dimmed.

Suggested Aroma Blend for Rappaccini's Daughter

Use the following blend of essential oils to create a sweet, exotic aroma that evokes the flower garden where Beatrice is confined and the scent of her breath.

30 drops of lavender essential oil
7 drops of geranium essential oil
42 drops of sweet orange essential oil
4 ounces of water

Fill a glass or plastic spray container with an ounce of water. Add the drops of lavender, geranium, and sweet orange and shake the mixture gently. Add the rest of the water and shake again. Spray as needed. The fragrance will remain in the air for about 15 minutes.

Warning

Be alert to the potential hazards of using certain essential oils, including allergic reactions. Essential oils are highly concentrated, so it is best to use a carrier such as water for spray. Sprays have a lesser impact than applications, but in higher concentrations they can cause irritation. Never substitute synthetics, because they can be toxic.

Be careful to avoid the essential oils listed below, which can cause allergic reactions for some people. Always be vigilant for any special health concerns of individual students.

Essential Oils with a Proven or Suspected History of Causing Sensitization

Aniseed	Junipers
Balsam	Laurel (bay laurel)
Balsam of Peru	Lemon**
Bay	Lemon Verbena
Benzoin	Litsea Cubeba**
Calamus	Lovage**
Cardamom	Mimosa Absolute
Cassia*	Oakmoss Concrete**
Cinnamon Bark & Leaf*	Orange**
Citronella	Pines**
Fennel	Rose Absolute*
Fig Leaf Absolute	Spearmint
Galbanum Resin***	Tolu
Hyacinth Absolute	Tagetes
Jasmine Absolute	Ylangylang*

*Use only at low concentrations
**Suspect
***When used with Balsam of Peru

Calligraphy

Goal: To provide motivation for writing

Calligraphy, derived from the Greek word for "beautiful writing," is visual art produced in simple strokes by a broad-tipped instrument or brush. It is usually cursive, though sometimes angular. At first glance, producing calligraphic writing may seem intimidating. But it is actually easy to get started. Calligraphic magic markers in various colors are readily available. So are books offering instruction in calligraphy *(see resource section on page 41)*, as well as guides on the Internet that are suitable for beginners. Special paper can add additional aesthetic dimensions. Use calligraphic fonts such as Calligula *(see example below)* when creating word-processed documents. Students' motivation to complete class projects should be enhanced as they seek an outlet for their new calligraphic skills.

Materials

Unlined 4" x 6" index cards, assorted colors or white
Calligraphy magic markers, assorted colors or black

Guidelines

Allow students time to practice with a calligraphy marker. With the index cards and calligraphy markers, let the students create Structured Poetry *(see pages 17–18)* about "Rappaccini's Daughter." This can make a lovely display in your classroom or school hallway.

> Flowers are growing
> Lovely purple fragrant blooms
> Do not believe them

Acrostic Poems

Goal: To enrich the study of characterization in literature

An Acrostic Poem uses the first, last, or other letters in each line to spell out a word or phrase in a vertical format. Use the names of characters in "Rappaccini's Daughter" to explore their personal attributes and ethical dilemmas, as exemplified below.

Materials

Paper and pen

Guidelines

Each line should say something meaningful about the character in question. Calligraphic lettering can be used manually or by word processor to embellish the visual appeal of the poem.

Glowing
In love
Over his head
Valiant but foolish
Always at the window
Nothing can deter him
Nothing can save him
Innocent love undone

Try using the middle letter in each line, as shown in the example below, to spell out a theme in the story. Or, for a real challenge, try using the last letter in each line.

Overcome with Longing
So near but yet sO far away
Trying in Vain but not letting go
ImpossiblE to imagine the end

Structured Poetry

Goals: To enjoy poetry; to experience success as a poet

Structured Poetry follows a predetermined pattern, such as prescribing the number of syllables per line, the number of lines per verse, or the parts of speech used. Yet these simple poetic forms can express complex ideas. Thus, they foster success in writing in meaningful ways for the novice poet. Structured Poetry can take the fear out of writing a poem, paving the way for students to understand and even experiment with free verse. It can also give students practice in writing succinctly and creatively. There is a multitude of structured poetic forms from which to choose, easily obtainable in print or over the Internet.

Materials

Paper and pen or pencil
Guidelines and examples *(see pages 17–18)*

Guidelines

Students can create poetic character portraits from multiple perspectives. For example, they could write poems about Beatrice, poems in Beatrice's voice, or poems in the voice of another character (say, Giovanni) expressing thoughts and feelings about Beatrice. Or they could create and publish their own poetry anthologies on the themes in "Rappaccini's Daughter," incorporating artwork and using book-making techniques. Poems should, of course, follow the correct structure and express coherent ideas.

For an illustration of how to use such poems in an Instant Accordion Book, see page 21.

Haiku

The *haiku* is based on a syllabic pattern expressed in three lines that convey a single idea. The first line contains five syllables, the second contains seven syllables, and the third contains five syllables.

Flowers are growing
Lovely purple fragrant blooms
Do not believe them

Haikon

The *haikon* is a pictorial representation of the haiku. For example, the poem above could be converted into a haikon by drawing a flower or its outline, then writing the words around its shape.

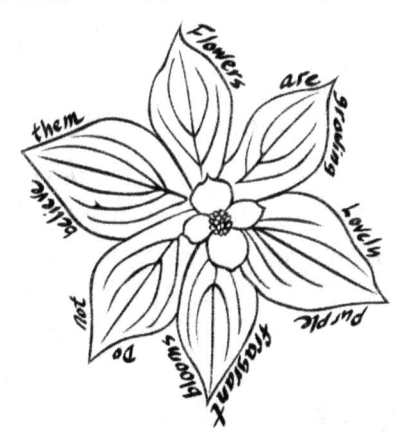

Tanka

The *tanka* adds two more lines to the haiku, each containing seven syllables.

Flowers are growing
Lovely purple fragrant blooms
Do not believe them
They beckon, they entice you
If you follow you are doomed

Terquain

The *terquain* uses structure—three lines on a single subject—without a rigid syllabic formula. So it offers students an easy way to become successful poets. The first line consists of a one-word noun. The second line describes the noun in two or three words, and the third line is either a synonym for the noun or describes a feeling about it.

Love
Falling, soaring, collapsing
Confusion

Cinquain

The *cinquain* also uses structure without a rigid syllabic formula, but it's a bit more sophisticated. The first line is a noun. The second line uses two words to describe the noun. The third line contains three action verbs that describe the noun, while the fourth line contains four words that describe feelings about the noun. The fifth and final line consists of one word that is synonymous with the noun used in the first line.

> *Daughter*
> *Kind, captive*
> *Imprisoned, sequestered, caged*
> *Sadness, melancholy, grief, longing*
> *Beatrice*

Diamante

The *diamante* combines grammatical structure with pictorial form in seven lines. It splits thematically in the fourth line, so that the first half of the poem is conceptually the opposite of the second half of the poem. It is graphically represented in a diamond shape.

> *Antidote*
> *warm, bright*
> *smile, laugh, dance*
> *remedy, cure, venom, toxicant*
> *shiver, tremble, crush*
> *cold, still*
> *poison*

As illustrated above, the first line consists of one word, a noun, and the last line is its opposite. The second and sixth lines contain two adjectives that describe the respective nouns. The third and fifth lines contain three action verbs each, and the fourth (middle) line is split, with two nouns referring to each opposing concept.

Script and Story Writing

Goals: To provide motivation for reading and writing

Many other stories are embedded before, after, and between the lines of "Rappaccini's Daughter." Pose these or similar questions to the students:

- What happened to Beatrice's mother?
- How did Beatrice and her father relate to each other when they were not in the garden?
- Who was Lisabetta and what other secrets did she carry?
- How did Doctor Rappaccini become a crazed botanist?
- What happened to Giovanni after he became poisonous and Beatrice died?
- How would the story change if Beatrice had not drunk the antidote, or if Giovanni had drunk it instead?
- What other stories are hidden within "Rappaccini's Daughter?"
- What would happen if the story of "Rappaccini's Daughter" were to be transposed to modern times?

All of these questions can be used as prompts for students to write original stories. Or they can write original scripts in small groups, making it a cooperative activity.

For an extension, students can stage dramatic readings of their stories or theatrical presentations of their scripts.

Materials

Paper, pen, word processor

Guidelines

It is important to avoid inhibiting student creativity and motivation by an overemphasis on rules of grammar and composition. Brainstorming ideas is a good way to begin, followed by free writing. Technical aspects of writing should be saved for the editing process, when the stories and scripts are nearing completion.

Script-Making

Flipping pages can be akward, especially in dramatic readings. One quick solution to this problem is to print scripts using the booklet format (a convenient feature of Adobe Acrobat PDFs), as shown beginning on page 145.

Instant Accordion Books

Goal: To motivate students to write through the creation of books as art objects

Book-making is an art form in its own right. Artists have been active in printing and book production for centuries, but Artist's Books are a late-20th-century form. Often published in small editions, these are sometimes produced as one-of-a-kind objects known as "uniques."

The book arts combine a wide range of formats and crafts. Formats can be as simple as a scroll or accordion book made from a single sheet of paper, or as complex as a hand-bound volume with embossed pages. The books students create may be kept in a classroom or school library or displayed for the school community at special events.

Making an Instant Accordion Book is an easy way to incorporate the book arts into activities on "Rappaccini's Daughter." Each page can highlight a structured poem that students have written about a character or theme from "Rappaccini's Daughter." See page 155 for an example template of an Instant Accordion Book.

Materials

One sheet of letter size (8.5" x 11") paper
Pen or calligraphy marker
Clear tape
Scissors (optional)
Ruler (optional)

Guidelines

This variation of an Instant Accordion Book was designed for quick classroom use with minimal effort and materials. All that is required is one sheet of paper, some tape, and a pen or calligraphy marker.

For directions on making a more elaborate accordion book, or for ideas on making more complex "uniques," see the Resource section on page 41.

Directions

1. Fold and cut the paper in half lengthwise. Or crease it at the fold several times, in opposite directions, so it will tear in half easily.

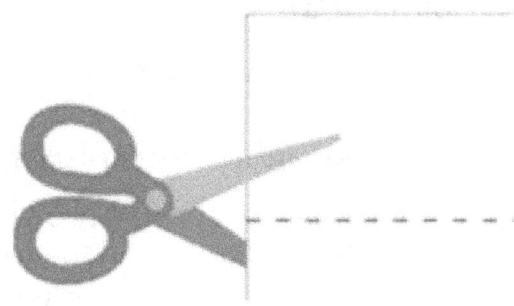

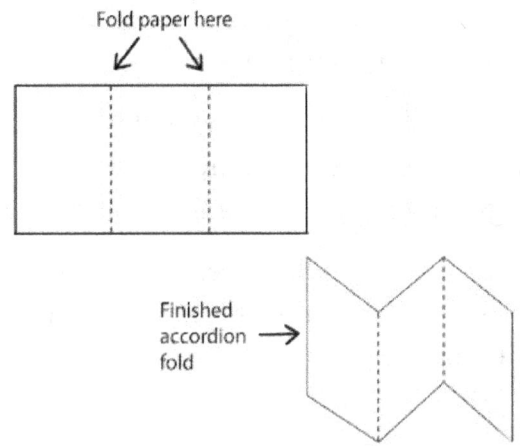

2. Fold each half in thirds (a ruler may be used, but is not necessary).

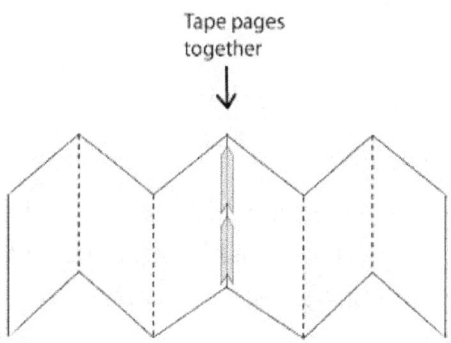

3. Tape the two pieces of paper together at the edges with clear tape. The edges should not overlap.

4. Write a structured poem on each page.

5. The final product can be used as a book or opened to create a long, flat rectangle that can be used to display all six poems.

6. See page 155 for a template that can be folded to create an example of an Instant Accordion Book. Students can use a calligraphy pen to write structured poems about "Rappaccini's Daughter" on each of the six pages.

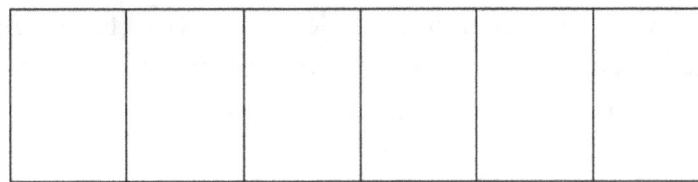

7. See page 159 for a template that already contains poems about the story.

Character Mind Maps

Goal: To give visual display to a literary character's cognitive process

A Mind Map is a visual display of information. Associated words, ideas, and concepts are written and connected by lines that radiate out from a central word, idea, or concept. Mind Maps may include illustrations, but they are not necessary.

A Character Mind Map, however, must include illustrations. The highlighted literary character appears in the center of the page and is surrounded by images and words that reflect his or her thoughts and feelings. Connective lines are not necessary.

Ask the students to illustrate how the world appears to Beatrice, to Doctor Rappaccini, to Giovanni, to Lisabetta, or to Baglioni. On the facing page is a Character Mind Map from the point of view of Giovanni.

Materials

Paper
Drawing supplies

Guidelines

A Character Mind Map should expand as it is being created. Brainstorming should happen not just beforehand but throughout the process. Writing an Acrostic Poem can be a good warm-up activity. For example, a poem about Giovanni could be the prelude to creating a Character Mind Map from his perspective, as in the drawing opposite. Although students should strive for engaging illustrations, it is the thought process behind the drawing, not the graphic sophistication that matters most.

Extension Activity: Character Mind Mural

A mural is any piece of artwork that is painted on or applied directly to a large permanent surface, such as a wall. It incorporates different pictures that are thematically related. Students can create a mural of the events in "Rappaccini's Daughter" from the point of view of one of the characters. Although similar to a Character Mind Map, the visual format is less restrictive (for example, images need not radiate out from a central concept). Text is not included. And a Character Mind Mural is well suited to a collective student activity.

Glenna A. Reyes

Character Self-Portrait

Goal: To explore the life experiences and feelings of a literary character

Create a self-portrait from the perspective of one of the characters in "Rappaccini's Daughter" expressing that individual's experiences and feelings. This can be done as a traditional representation that is drawn or painted. Since some students lack confidence in their drawing ability, you might suggest other artistic mediums such as photography, sculpture, or collage. Or be inventive and try something completely different, such as a mobile or a musical arrangement that captures the essence of one of the characters.

Materials

Writing
Art or music supplies as needed

Guidelines

Begin by discussing the sounds and/or images that students would choose to express their own personalities. Then discuss the sounds and/or images that could express the various characters in "Rappaccini's Daughter." Acrostic Poems and Character Mind Maps can also be used as warm-up activities. The process of character exploration is more important than the finished product, but students should put serious effort into creating a work that they can feel proud of.

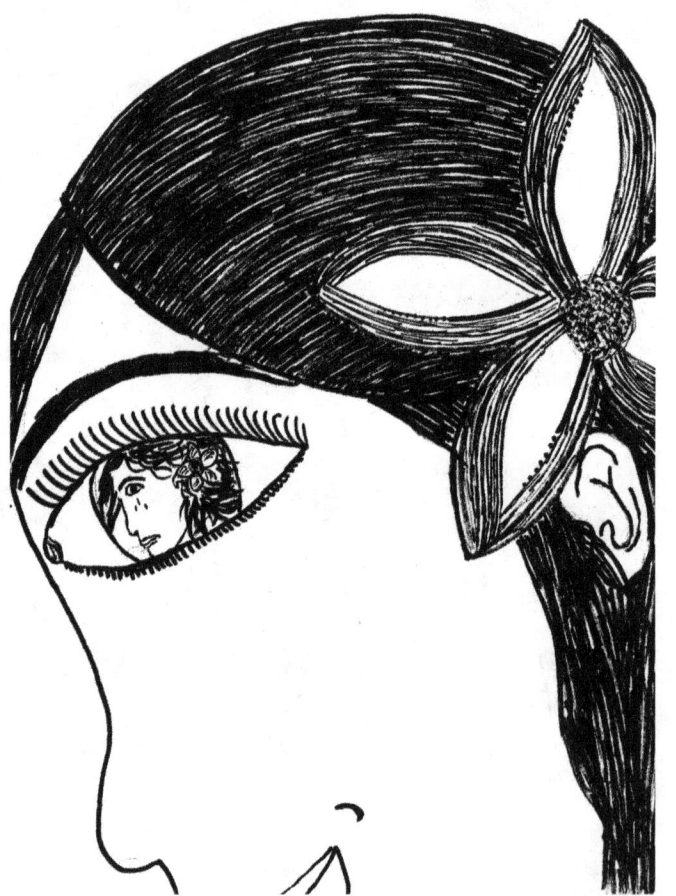

Glenna A. Reyes

Jazz Chants

Goal: To enjoy key concepts in a literary work by setting them to rhythm and movement

Carolyn Graham, the creator of Jazz Chants for use in teaching English as a second language, defines them as "poems with repeated beats" using simple language that is real, purposeful, and appropriate for the learner. They are the "rhythmic expression of spoken American English [that can be used as] a way of learning to speak and understand with special attention to the sound system of a language." For all of these reasons, Jazz Chants are especially useful with English learners.

As their name suggests, Jazz Chants originated with the musical genre of jazz, which in turn can be traced back to the West African musical style that incorporates polyrhythms (the simultaneous combination of contrasting rhythms), syncopation, improvisation, and call-and-response. Jazz Chants are frequently used in English learner classrooms because they use the motivational elements of movement and rhythm to scaffold the syllable stress and intonation of conversational American English.

Graham became interested in Jazz Chants when she realized that "the sound of spoken language reflects exactly the rhythm of traditional American jazz." It made sense to her to use Jazz Chants to teach ESL, because doing so "brought rhythm into the classroom, and the brain loves rhythm." She points out that rhythm and memory are closely linked, noting that "a student can easily memorize any material if you present it with rhythm."

Today Jazz Chant competitions are held throughout the world. Many of these teacher- and student-created routines are easily accessible on YouTube. As can be seen by the diverse ages of the competitors, Jazz Chants are enjoyable to students from primary through secondary school. See page 40 of the Resource section for more detailed information on how to create a Jazz Chant.

Materials

None required; costume pieces and props optional

Guidelines

Create a Jazz Chant in a 4/4 tempo about "Rappaccini's Daughter" *(see example on the next page)* incorporating hand-clapping, foot-stamping and/or simple body movements. In addition to maintaining a jazz beat, the students should be using language that is real, purposeful, and appropriate for everyday purposes.

Jazz Chant for "Rappaccini's Daughter"
(Chanted in 4/4 Rhythm)

There's a flower,
[Clap] Don't touch it!
And there's a twig,
[Clap] Don't touch it!
And there's a shrub,
[Clap] Don't touch it!
If you [spoken in one syncopated beat] want to live!
[Pause, clap, clap, clap]

Rhythm Chart

Beat One	Beat Two	Beat Three	Beat Four
There's	a	flow-	er,
[Clap]	Don't	touch	it!
And	there's	a	twig,
[Clap]	Don't	touch	it!
And	there's	a	shrub,
[Clap]	Don't	touch	it!
If you	want	to	live!
[Silence]	[Clap]	[Clap]	[Clap]

Rap

Goals: To appreciate and create poetry; to understand poetry as a contemporary and relevant art form

Rap is poetry set to a musical beat. Grounded in popular culture, it often has immediate appeal for adolescents. Rhyming lyrics are chanted to musical accompaniment and performed in time to an insistent, recurring rhythm. Rap is heavily dependent on lyrics and has a strong background in improvisational poetry.

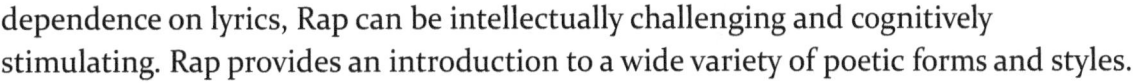

Contrary to popular belief, Rap is also a highly structured musical form. Its reliance on patterned lyrics makes it a form of Structured Poetry as well. Due to the complexity of that structure, however, it is most appropriate for use with secondary students. Because of its strong dependence on lyrics, Rap can be intellectually challenging and cognitively stimulating. Rap provides an introduction to a wide variety of poetic forms and styles.

The appropriate use of Rap as a classroom genre illustrates for students how language can be both relevant and playful and how word play is enjoyable. And remember—it's all about the lyrics.

Materials

Handouts on rhyme, metaphor, and structure of a Rap
Sample audio recordings with written transcript of lyrics (optional)
Metronome to help students maintain the beat (optional)
Electronic keyboard or other musical equipment for base beat (optional)

Guidelines

Appearances can be deceiving; Rap is a complex genre. Do not attempt to incorporate Rap into your classroom without some technical grounding in this contemporary art form *(see page 167 for assistance)*. After practice with the features of Rap, take a look at "Rappaccini's Rap" beginning on page 175 and try to find the Rap features contained within. Then let the students create their own Rap, based on a theme, character, or the action in the story. As an extension, let them create their own music video and share it with the class. The finished Raps should adhere to structural guidelines and have a consistent rhythm. Their artistry will be evident in the quality of the lyrics, for example, the use of rhyme scheme and metaphor.

Part II
Teacher Resources

Readers Theater
Production Notes
Follow–Up Activities
Strategy Progressions

Historical and Literary Background
Nathaniel Hawthorne and Tomaso Albinoni
Origins of "Rappaccini's Daughter"
Adaptations of Hawthorne's Story

Reference Materials
Dramatic Arts
Readers Theater
Aromas to Evoke Mood
Greek Chorus
Jazz Chants
Book Arts
Accordion Books
Calligraphy
Fine Arts in Spanish
Creative Arts Activities for English Language Learners
Hawthorne

Production Notes

Casting Suggestions

Cast two characters in each role and rotate the cast. This will maximize participation and also provide understudies in case of student absence. To involve every student in the production, consider the use of a tech crew and a Greek Chorus.

Suggested Aroma Blend

Use the blend of essential oils found on page 12 to create a sweet, exotic aroma that evokes the flower garden where Beatrice is confined. Spray the essential oil blend into the air between the appropriate scenes while the lights are dimmed. Vary the amount of spray used as the performance reaches its conclusion. Begin with a subtle aroma and end with an intense sweetness.

PowerPoint Slides

Ask the students to look for images to use in each scene. This can be done as simply as searching the Internet, but can be as elaborate as creating original backdrops that can be photographed and copied into PowerPoint slides. A number of the scenes use the same setting, so there is no need to create seven unique backdrops. Beginning and ending PowerPoint slides can also be designed that display the title of the production, the cast and credits, and so on.

Suggested Music

"Adagio for Strings and Organ in G Minor," by Tomaso Albinoni, which can be embedded in the PowerPoint slides to automatically play during scene breaks.

The following recording is especially evocative: *Albinoni: Adagio / Pachelbel: Canon,* performed by the Orpheus Chamber Orchestra (Deutsche Grammophon, 1991).

List of Characters and Staging Suggestions

See Readers Theater scripts in Part III.

Follow-Up Activities

- Turn your classroom into a theater for staging multiple productions. Invite other classrooms to attend.

- Make a program book for the performance. You may want to include historical information about the original story and its author, along with short bios of the performers.

- Read the original story *(see Part III)* and compare it to a Readers Theater script.

- View the PBS film of "Rappaccini's Daughter." Contrast the film to the original literature and to a Readers Theater script. Critique the film.

- Stage the Theatrical Production beginning on page 131.

- Create a movie trailer for "Rappaccini's Daughter."

- Research and view or read other works of art based on "Rappaccini's Daughter" *(see pages 38–39)*.

- Research the traditional Indian folktale and other literature that inspired Hawthorne to write "Rappaccini's Daughter" *(see pages 37–38)*. Discuss how works such as *Romeo and Juliet* have been updated to become contemporary. Then let the students create a story, script, or a performance transposing "Rappaccini's Daughter" into modern times.

- Explore character motives. For example, what was actually in the vial that Baglioni gave Giovanni? Did he know it would kill Beatrice? Did he imagine that Giovanni might drink it? Would it have killed him if he did? How much did Lisabetta know about Doctor Rappaccini's plan? Did she realize that Giovanni could become poisonous? How did she feel when she learned the result of her complicity?

- Discuss questions raised by the story, such as:
  - What is ethical in the name of scientific research?
  - Do ends justify means?
  - Is love blind? How can we learn to distinguish love from infatuation?
  - How can once-healthy relationships be figuratively poisoned by others?
  - How do fantasy and reality work together and against each other to shape one's perceptions?

Strategy Progressions

The strategies in this book can be combined in a progression leading to a culminating activity. Three possible sequences (Options One, Two, and Three) are described below, but many more are possible, depending on the classroom and teaching context. Note that all three options begin in the same way—with a Readers Theater production of "Rappaccini's Daughter"—after which the unit can branch off in one of three directions. Finally, all three options end in the same way, with a reading of Hawthorne's original story.

Goals

In the short term, students should experience "Rappaccini's Daughter" for understanding and meaning, and connect its themes to their own experiences. The long-term goal of appreciating literature will be more difficult to evaluate. Enjoying the Readers Theater experience, however, will be an important step in that direction.

Possible Thematic Connections

History • Literature • Science • Ethics

Materials (all options)

Readers Theater scripts
Symbolic props and costumes
Essential oil spray
PowerPoint background slides
Audio equipment or music-embedded PowerPoints
Writing tools

Additional Materials (Option One: Greek Chorus)

Robes for Greek Chorus

Additional Materials (Option Two: Poetry and Visual Art)

Calligraphy markers or pens
Index cards
Supplies to create Artist's Books, Character Mind Maps, and Character Self-Portraits

Additional Materials (Option Three: Rap)

For students (see page 167):
  Parts of a Rap
  Structure of a Rap
  Metaphor and Rhyme in Rap
  Suggested Process for Creating a Rap
  "Rappaccini's Rap"

For teachers (see pages 179–181):
  Exploring "Rappaccini's Rap"
  "Rappaccini's Rap" Answer Key

Metronome to help students maintain the beat (optional)
Electronic keyboard or other musical equipment for base beat (optional)
Video equipment

Opening (for Options One, Two, and Three)

Ask students the following question and discuss their answers: *What would you do if you fell in love and then discovered the person you had fallen in love with was actually (literally, not figuratively) poisonous?*

Explain that this dilemma was the basis for a short story by Nathaniel Hawthorne. Then provide background information about the author and his times *(see page 36)*, which will flow naturally into the Readers Theater script.

Choose a script for "Rappaccini's Daughter" *(see Part III)*. Give each student a copy and time to read silently. (Or send the scripts home to be read before the next class.) Discuss the story, then ask for volunteers for specific roles.

Clear a space in the classroom for the characters to sit in accordance with their relationships to, and interactions with, each other *(see staging directions in Part III)*.

Distribute symbolic props and costume pieces. Do multiple readings of the script, rotating characters to ensure everyone has a chance to participate.

Turn the classroom into a theater and prepare to stage multiple productions, so that roles can be filled by various students.

Students who choose not to play characters can assist in other ways, such as ushering, creating props and costumes, researching and creating PowerPoint slides for use as scene backdrops, or producing a program booklet. The booklet can include historical information about the original story and its author, as well as short biographies of the cast and crew.

Evoke an aura of mystery by playing music *(see page 30)* and dimming the lights between scenes.

Use backdrops with projected PowerPoint images that the students have found or created.

Before the beginning of scenes that incorporate the scent of poisonous flowers, spray a sweet floral essential oil in the air *(see page 12)* while the lights are off.

Invite other classrooms to attend. Hawthorne can be difficult. The production can make literature both accessible and enjoyable for other students.

The unit can end at this point, or it could go off in three directions, as described below.

Option One

Explore the themes in "Rappaccini's Daughter" through the use of a Greek Chorus.

Discuss critical issues brought forward by the story, such as "What is ethical in the name of scientific research?" and "Do ends justify means?" Have students compose the lines for a Greek Chorus to add to the appropriate Readers Theater script based on these issues *(see pages 8–9)*. Develop the work into a performance for another class. Then invite that class to collectively discuss with your own students the moral or ethical issues raised in the performance.

Option Two

Explore the characters and themes in "Rappaccini's Daughter" through poetry and visual art.

Write Acrostic Poems about the characters *(see page 15)*.

Create structured poems on the theme of the story or from the perspective of one of the characters *(see pages 17–18)*.

Write the poems using calligraphy *(see page 14)*.

Create a Character Mind Map from the perspective of one of the characters in the story, for example, Giovanni's conflicting views of Beatrice or Beatrice's thought process regarding her father *(see page 23)*.

Create a Character Self-Portrait from the perspective of a character in the story *(see page 24)*.

Create an interpretive book about the story using Acrostic Poems, Structured Poetry, Character Mind Maps, and Character Self-Portraits. Divide the students into cooperative groups and ask them to produce one Artist's Book ("unique") per group. The groups can be offered choices in book types, or they can all make the same variety *(see page 41 for ideas)*.

Option Three

Explore the characters and themes in "Rappaccini's Daughter" through the use of Rap.

Ask the students what they know about the genre of Rap, then use the handouts beginning on page 167 to explain the form and features of a Rap.

In cooperative groups, read "Rappaccini's Rap" *(see page 175)* and discuss the meaning of these original lyrics. Then look for metaphors and rhyme forms within the Rap.

Students who are interested in performing the Rap may practice within their group.

Cooperative groups share their discussions with the entire class. Students who have practiced the Rap may perform it for the class.

Each group composes an original Rap based on "Rappaccini's Daughter," rehearses it, and creates a Rap video. Props and costumes can be included. Roles can be divided within the group, so that those who do not want to perform are not forced to do so. All of the videos are viewed by the students and could even be shared with other classrooms or at a school special event.

Unit Conclusion (for Options One, Two, and Three)

Think back to the opening question: *What would you do if you fell in love and then discovered the person you had fallen in love with was actually poisonous?*

Would you now change your answer, or leave it the same? What are your reasons?

Read Hawthorne's original story. (Although initially it would have been difficult for the students to comprehend, after so much practice with its elements this should no longer be the case.)

Compare the original story to the Reader's Theater version.

Note that the original story *(reprinted in Part III)* is divided to correspond with the scenes in the Readers Theater version. This should make the comparison easier and could also help guide the students into creating their own stories.

Discuss Hawthorne's writing style in the context of his times.

Individually or in cooperative groups, write a modern version of "Rappaccini's Daughter." Share the resulting stories with the entire class.

Historical and Literary Background

Nathaniel Hawthorne (1804–1864)

Nathaniel Hawthorne is best known for his novel *The Scarlet Letter*, completed in 1850, but he also wrote more than a hundred short stories, sketches, children's stories, novels, and nonfiction pieces. Among his best known stories is "Rappaccini's Daughter," first published in *The United States Magazine and Democratic Review* in 1844. Two years later it was included in his short story collection *Mosses from an Old Manse*. Although it is set in Padua, Italy, the narrative is most likely adapted from a folktale originating in India.

Hawthorne was born on July 4, 1804 in Salem, Massachusetts and lived there for much of his life. The events of 1692 in Salem haunted him, especially as his great-grandfather was a judge in the witchcraft trials.

It was in Salem, too, where Hawthorne met Sophia Peabody. They married on July 9, 1842. The Hawthornes moved in Concord, but returned to Salem late in 1845. They left again in 1850, to live over the years in several other locales. Although they never returned, Salem continued to influence Hawthorne's life, as it remained the setting for many of his literary works.

Hawthorne was in failing health during his final years. He died in his sleep on May 18, 1864.

Tomaso Albinoni (1671–1751)

Tomaso Albinoni was an Italian composer of Baroque music, including 81 operas, 99 sonatas, 59 concertos, 50 operas, and nine symphonies. Although he is widely known today for his oboe concertos, this Italian composer was principally a violinist.

The Baroque style of European classical music was popular between 1600 and 1750, the era during which the action in "Rappaccini's Daughter" more than likely took place. Other important composers of Baroque music include Johann Sebastian Bach, George Frederick Handel, Antonio Vivaldi, and Johann Pachelbel.

Origins of "Rappaccini's Daughter"

The origin of Hawthorne's story, in all likelihood, lies in the mythological Vish Kanya, or Poison Girl. The theme of a woman transformed into a living body of venom is not uncommon in Indian literature and dates as far back as the ancient Hindu religious texts known as *The Puranas*.

In traditional tales, Visha Kanya (plural of Vish Kanya) were created by exposing young girls to low levels of poison, a practice called mithridatism. The outcome was either death or immunity. Those who developed immunity were believed to have poisonous body fluids which would be lethal to other humans. As such, they were said to have sometimes been used as living weapons.

The historical play, *Mudrarakshasa*, originally written in Sanskrit by Vishakhadatta, is such a tale. Written somewhere between the 4th and 8th centuries, it tells of political intrigue between two rivals, one of whom employs a Vish Kanya as a beautiful assassin in his quest for power.

As time passed, the Visha Kanya became an archetype, passing from folklore to popular culture. From classical Sanskrit texts such as the *Sukasaptati* to modern works of fiction like Vishkanya by the popular Hindi writer Shivani (1923–2003), the character of the Poison Girl has long been present in Indian literature and culture. From India she traveled to the West, making an appearance in *Gesta Romanorum*, a Latin collection of anecdotes and tales, and then eventually took the form of Beatrice Rappaccini.

The *Gesta Romanorum (Deeds of the Romans)* was originally written somewhere near the end of the 13th and the beginning of the 14th centuries. Its authorship is not clear, but its purpose was; it was meant for use by clergy. Its moralistic themes contained fragments of stories whose origins ranged from Asia to Europe. It is theorized that these elements were the seeds of many literary works written by such notable figures as Geoffrey Chaucer and William Shakespeare. Hawthorne may have borrowed from the volume as well—specifically from an anecdote that can be traced back to the Vish Kanya. In it, an Indian Queen sends her exquisitely beautiful daughter as a gift to Alexander the Great. Aristotle warns Alexander in time to avert a tragedy, as the girl is a Vish Kanya, and touching her lips would have meant certain death.

The story of the poisonous maiden resurfaced in 1621, with the publication of Robert Burton's *The Anatomy of Melancholy*, which included the story of the Indian king Porus, who sends a poisonous girl to Alexander the Great. In the 1800s this same story inspired still other writers. It gave Oliver Wendell Holmes the inspiration for *Elsie Venner: A Romance of Destiny* (1861), the story of a woman who is half-woman and half-snake because her mother had been bitten by a rattlesnake while pregnant. Richard Garnett, likewise, was inspired by this tale when he created the short story "The Poison Maid," found in his book *The Twilight of the Gods and Other Tales* (1903). The heroine, interestingly named Mithridata, is raised from infancy on poisons of various kinds, from snake venom to compounds such as arsenic and strychnine. (Luckily for her, her future suitor has been raised on its antidotes. The same happy ending was denied to Elsie Venner.)

Although it is not clear just how much of the history of the Vish Kanya was known to Hawthorne, he must minimally have been aware of Burton's portrayal of her in *The Anatomy of Melancholy*, as the same story is recounted by Professor Pietro Baglioni to Giovanni Guasconti in "Rappaccini's Daughter."

Adaptations of Hawthorne's Story

Television
"Rappaccini's Daughter" on PBS's *American Short Story*, starring Kristoffer Tabori, and Kathleen Beller (1980). See http://www.imdb.com/title/tt0081403/.

Film
Twice Told Tales, starring Vincent Price (United Artists, 1963); based on three literary works by Nathaniel Hawthorne, one of which is "Rappaccini's Daughter." Available at https://www.youtube.com/watch?v=RULBBg6kP38.

Theater
La Hija de Rappaccini (in Spanish), by Octavio Paz (1956).
Rappaccini's Daughter, by Sebastian Doggart (1996).

Opera
Rappaccini's Daughter, by Charles Wakefield Cadman (premiered in 1925).
Rappaccini's Daughter, by Margaret Garwood (premiered in 1983).
La hija de Rappaccini, by Daniel Catán (premiered in 1991); based on the play by Octavio Paz.
The Poisoned Kiss, or The Empress and the Necromancer, by Ralph Vaughan Williams, libretto by Evelyn Sharp (premiered in 1936); based on both Richard Garnett's *The Poison Maid* and *Nathaniel Hawthorne's Rappaccini's Daughter.*

Song
"Running through the Garden" by Stevie Nicks, Gary Nicholson, and Ray Kennedy; track #11 on the Fleetwood Mac album *Say You Will* (Reprise, 2003).

HISTORICAL & LITERARY BACKGROUND

Musical Play

Beautiful Poison; music by Brendan Milburn, lyrics by Valerie Vagoda, and book by Duane Poole (2014). The setting has been changed to New Orleans; the music combines contemporary rock, jazz funerals, and Dixieland styles with voodoo rhythms.

Poetry

The Poison-Flower, A Phantasy, in Three Scenes; a verse-play by John Todhunter (1891).

Radio

NBC's *The Weird Circle* (1943–1947), Episode 52, "Rappaccini's Daughter"; radio play adaptation. Available at http://ia600508.us.archive.org/6/items/Weird_Circle_otr/Weird_Circle_-_441126_-_52_-_Rapacinis_Daughter_-_32-22_25m09s_5897.mp3

Readers Theater

"Rappaccini's Daughter" script adapted by Jennifer L. Kroll in *Classic Readers Theatre for Young Adults* (2002; *see page 40 for citation*).

Comics

DC Comics character Poison Ivy is partly inspired by Hawthorne's story.

Marvel Comics Universe character, Monica Rappaccini, is a biochemical genius and a villain. Her daughter Thasanee Rappaccini (known as Carmilla Black) is immune to poison but poisonous to others.

Reference Materials

Dramatic Arts

Viola Spolin. *Improvisation for the Theatre: A Handbook of Teaching and Directing Techniques.* Evanston, IL: Northwestern University Press, 1999.

> A classic that has influenced the fields of education, mental health, social work, and psychology; it includes many activities that can be adapted by creative educators.

_____. *Theatre Games for the Classroom: A Teacher's Handbook.* Evanston, IL: Northwestern University Press, 1986.

> Includes improvisational techniques and games that are designed specifically for classroom use. Their purpose is to increase self-awareness while teaching the basic elements of storytelling, literary criticism, and character analysis.

Readers Theater

Suzanne I. Barchers and Jennifer L. Kroll. *Classic Readers Theatre for Young Adults.* Greenwood Village, CO: Teachers Ideas Press, 2002.

> Features Readers Theater scripts adapted from classic literature in the public domain, along with stage production ideas.

Aromas to Evoke Mood

Kathi Keville and Mindy Green. *Aroma Therapy: A Complete Guide to the Healing Art.* Berkeley, CA: Crossing Press, 2009.

> A comprehensive introduction to aromatherapy, including a list of essential oils that are commonly available, along with techniques for blending and using them.

Greek Chorus

An excellent overview of Greek theater and the role of the Greek Chorus by N.S. Gill can be found at ancienthistory.about.com/od/greekliterature/a/GreekTheater.htm.

Jazz Chants

Catherine Graham. *Jazz Chants.* New York: Oxford University Press, 1978.

> Compiled by a pioneer in the adaption of Jazz Chants for teaching English as a second language. To order Graham's books, audio CDs, and audiobooks, visit her website at jazzchants.net/who-is-carolyn-graham.

Book Arts

Here are some titles that contain creative ideas and instructions on book-making:

Linda Fry Kenzle. *Pages: Innovative Bookmaking Techniques.* Iola, WI: Krause Publications, 1998.

Alisa Golden. *Making Handmade Books: 100 + Bindings, Structures & Forms.* New York: Lark Crafts, 2011.

Heather Weston. *Bookcraft: Techniques for Binding, Folding, and Decorating to Create Books and More.* Beverly, MA: Quarry Books, 2008.

Accordion Books

See http://maskedpixie.blogspot.com/2011/09/bookmaking-with-masked-pixie-part-3.html

Calligraphy

Don Marsh. *Calligraphy.* Cincinnati, OH: North Light Books, 1996.

Among the many books available on calligraphy, this one is an excellent way to get beginners started.

Fine Arts in Spanish

Sharon Adelman Reyes, Salvador Gabaldón, and José Severo Morejón (Eds.). *La Palabra Justa: A Glossary for K–12 Bilingual Teachers.* Portland, OR: DiversityLearningK12, 2014.

A Spanish-English/English-Spanish glossary featuring terms from academic content areas, technology, and school life, along with extensive coverage of literature and the visual and performing arts.

Creative Arts Activities for English Learners

Sharon Adelman Reyes. *Engage the Creative Arts: A Framework of Sheltering and Scaffolding Instruction for English Language Learners.* Portland, OR: DiversityLearningK12, 2013.

A framework and corresponding ideas for using the creative arts in second language acquisition in grades K–12.

Hawthorne

For additional information on the life, times, and literary work of Nathaniel Hawthorne, visit http://www.hawthorneinsalem.org/.

Part III
Reproducibles

"Rappaccini's Daughter"
Story Synopsis
Original Story by Nathaniel Hawthorne

Scripts
Readers Theater, Secondary Level
Readers Theater with Greek Chorus, Secondary Level
Readers Theater, Middle School Level
Readers Theater with Greek Chorus, Basic Level
Theater, Secondary Level
Theater, Secondary Level (Booklet Format)

Handouts
Accordion Book Template
Accordion Book Template with Poetry
Jazz Chant
How to Write a Rap
"Rappaccini's Rap"
Exploring "Rappaccini's Rap" (Teacher Reference)
"Rappaccini's Rap" Answer Key

STORY SYNOPSIS

A young man, Giovanni Guasconti, moves to Padua to attend the university there and obtains a room overlooking Doctor Rappaccini's lush, locked garden. From this vantage point Giovanni is able to view the lovely Beatrice, who is confined within, as she tends her father's plants. He gains entrance to the garden through a housekeeper who has a key to the locked gate. There he meets and falls in love with the mysterious Beatrice.

Giovanni eventually notices Beatrice's unusual and intimate relationship with the plants in the garden. He sees fresh flowers wither and insects die when exposed to her breath. His mentor, Professor Pietro Baglioni, warns Giovanni that Rappaccini is not to be trusted. But, having fallen in love with Beatrice, Giovanni does not heed his advice.

Soon Giovanni begins to notice the consequences of his association with Beatrice. He must admit that she is poisonous and he is becoming poisonous as well. In the meantime, Baglioni gives Giovanni a vial, saying that it contains an antidote for Beatrice's poison.

Giovanni confronts Beatrice with his new knowledge of her nature, and she urges him to look past her poisonous exterior to see her pure and innocent essence. Giovanni produces the vial filled with the antidote, to share it with Beatrice, so they will be able to stay together. Beatrice grabs the vial from him, so as to check its safety by drinking it first. But, as poison has been her life, the only antidote is death. Beatrice dies in the garden, as Rappaccini looks on.

"Rappaccini's Daughter"
by Nathaniel Hawthorne

[Scene 1]*

A YOUNG MAN, named Giovanni Guasconti, came, very long ago, from the more southern region of Italy, to pursue his studies at the University of Padua. Giovanni, who had but a scanty supply of gold ducats in his pocket, took lodgings in a high and gloomy chamber of an old edifice, which looked not unworthy to have been the palace of a Paduan noble, and which, in fact, exhibited over its entrance the armorial bearings of a family long since extinct. The young stranger, who was not unstudied in the great poem of his country, recollected that one of the ancestors of this family, and perhaps an occupant of this very mansion, had been pictured by Dante as a partaker of the immortal agonies of his Inferno. These reminiscences and associations, together with the tendency to heart-break natural to a young man for the first time out of his native sphere, caused Giovanni to sigh heavily, as he looked around the desolate and ill-furnished apartment.

"Holy Virgin, signor," cried old dame Lisabetta, who, won by the youth's remarkable beauty of person, was kindly endeavoring to give the chamber a habitable air, "what a sigh was that to come out of a young man's heart! Do you find this old mansion gloomy? For the love of heaven, then, put your head out of the window, and you will see as bright sunshine as you have left in Naples."

Guasconti mechanically did as the old woman advised, but could not quite agree with her that the Lombard sunshine was as cheerful as that of southern Italy. Such as it was, however, it fell upon a garden beneath the window, and expended its fostering influences on a variety of plants, which seemed to have been cultivated with exceeding care.

"Does this garden belong to the house?" asked Giovanni.

"Heaven forbid, signor!—unless it were fruitful of better pot-herbs than any that grow there now," answered old Lisabetta. "No; that garden is cultivated by the own hands of Signor Giacomo Rappaccini, the famous Doctor, who, I warrant him, has been heard of as far as Naples. It is said he distils these plants into medicines that are as potent as a charm. Oftentimes you may see the Signor Doctor at work, and perchance the Signora his daughter, too, gathering the strange flowers that grow in the garden."

The old woman had now done what she could for the aspect of the chamber, and, commending the young man to the protection of the saints, took her departure.

Giovanni still found no better occupation than to look down into the garden beneath his window. From its appearance, he judged it to be one of those botanic gardens, which were of

*Scene breaks have been added to Hawthorne's original text to highlight story structure and to illustrate how the Readers Theater script was created.

earlier date in Padua than elsewhere in Italy, or in the world. Or, not improbably, it might once have been the pleasure-place of an opulent family; for there was the ruin of a marble fountain in the centre, sculptured with rare art, but so wofully shattered that it was impossible to trace the original design from the chaos of remaining fragments. The water, however, continued to gush and sparkle into the sunbeams as cheerfully as ever. A little gurgling sound ascended to the young man's window, and made him feel as if a fountain were an immortal spirit, that sung its song unceasingly, and without heeding the vicissitudes around it; while one century embodied it in marble, and another scattered the perishable garniture on the soil. All about the pool into which the water subsided, grew various plants, that seemed to require a plentiful supply of moisture for the nourishment of gigantic leaves, and, in some instances, flowers gorgeously magnificent. There was one shrub in particular, set in a marble vase in the midst of the pool, that bore a profusion of purple blossoms, each of which had the lustre and richness of a gem; and the whole together made a show so resplendent that it seemed enough to illuminate the garden, even had there been no sunshine. Every portion of the soil was peopled with plants and herbs, which, if less beautiful, still bore tokens of assiduous care; as if all had their individual virtues, known to the scientific mind that fostered them. Some were placed in urns, rich with old carving, and others in common garden-pots; some crept serpent-like along the ground, or climbed on high, using whatever means of ascent was offered them. One plant had wreathed itself round a statue of Vertumnus, which was thus quite veiled and shrouded in a drapery of hanging foliage, so happily arranged that it might have served a sculptor for a study.

While Giovanni stood at the window, he heard a rustling behind a screen of leaves, and became aware that a person was at work in the garden. His figure soon emerged into view, and showed itself to be that of no common laborer, but a tall, emaciated, sallow, and sickly looking man, dressed in a scholar's garb of black. He was beyond the middle term of life, with gray hair, a thin gray beard, and a face singularly marked with intellect and cultivation, but which could never, even in his more youthful days, have expressed much warmth of heart.

Nothing could exceed the intentness with which this scientific gardener examined every shrub which grew in his path; it seemed as if he was looking into their inmost nature, making observations in regard to their creative essence, and discovering why one leaf grew in this shape, and another in that, and wherefore such and such flowers differed among themselves in hue and perfume. Nevertheless, in spite of the deep intelligence on his part, there was no approach to intimacy between himself and these vegetable existences. On the contrary, he avoided their actual touch, or the direct inhaling of their odors, with a caution that impressed Giovanni most disagreeably; for the man's demeanor was that of one walking among malignant influences, such as savage beasts, or deadly snakes, or evil spirits, which, should he allow them one moment of license, would wreak upon him some terrible fatality. It was strangely frightful to the young man's imagination, to see this air of insecurity in a person cultivating a garden, that most simple and innocent of human toils, and which had been alike the joy and labor of the unfallen parents of the race. Was this garden, then, the Eden of the present world?—and this man, with such a perception of harm in what his own hands caused to grow, was he the Adam?

The distrustful gardener, while plucking away the dead leaves or pruning the too luxuriant growth of the shrubs, defended his hands with a pair of thick gloves. Nor were these his only armor. When, in his walk through the garden, he came to the magnificent plant that hung its purple gems beside the marble fountain, he placed a kind of mask over his mouth and nostrils, as if all this beauty did but conceal a deadlier malice. But finding his task still too dangerous, he drew back, removed the mask, and called loudly, but in the infirm voice of a person affected with inward disease:

"Beatrice!—Beatrice!"

"Here am I, my father! What would you?" cried a rich and youthful voice from the window of the opposite house; a voice as rich as a tropical sunset, and which made Giovanni, though he knew not why, think of deep hues of purple or crimson, and of perfumes heavily delectable.— "Are you in the garden?"

"Yes, Beatrice," answered the gardener, "and I need your help."

Soon there emerged from under a sculptured portal the figure of a young girl, arrayed with as much richness of taste as the most splendid of the flowers, beautiful as the day, and with a bloom so deep and vivid that one shade more would have been too much. She looked redundant with life, health, and energy; all of which attributes were bound down and compressed, as it were, and girdled tensely, in their luxuriance, by her virgin zone. Yet Giovanni's fancy must have grown morbid, while he looked down into the garden; for the impression which the fair stranger made upon him was as if here were another flower, the human sister of those vegetable ones, as beautiful as they—more beautiful than the richest of them—but still to be touched only with a glove, nor to be approached without a mask. As Beatrice came down the garden-path, it was observable that she handled and inhaled the odor of several of the plants, which her father had most sedulously avoided.

"Here, Beatrice," said the latter,—"see how many needful offices require to be done to our chief treasure. Yet, shattered as I am, my life might pay the penalty of approaching it so closely as circumstances demand. Henceforth, I fear, this plant must be consigned to your sole charge."

"And gladly will I undertake it," cried again the rich tones of the young lady, as she bent towards the magnificent plant, and opened her arms as if to embrace it. "Yes, my sister, my splendor, it shall be Beatrice's task to nurse and serve thee; and thou shalt reward her with thy kisses and perfume breath, which to her is as the breath of life!"

Then, with all the tenderness in her manner that was so strikingly expressed in her words, she busied herself with such attentions as the plant seemed to require; and Giovanni, at his lofty window, rubbed his eyes, and almost doubted whether it were a girl tending her favorite flower, or one sister performing the duties of affection to another. The scene soon terminated. Whether Doctor Rappaccini had finished his labors in the garden, or that his watchful eye had caught the stranger's face, he now took his daughter's arm and retired. Night was already closing in; oppressive exhalations seemed to proceed from the plants, and steal upward past the open window; and Giovanni, closing the lattice, went to his couch, and dreamed of a rich flower and beautiful girl. Flower and maiden were different and yet the same, and fraught with some strange peril in either shape.

[Scene 2]

BUT THERE IS AN INFLUENCE in the light of morning that tends to rectify whatever errors of fancy, or even of judgment, we may have incurred during the sun's decline, or among the shadows of the night, or in the less wholesome glow of moonshine. Giovanni's first movement on starting from sleep, was to throw open the window, and gaze down into the garden which his dreams had made so fertile of mysteries. He was surprised, and a little ashamed, to find how real and matter-of-fact an affair it proved to be, in the first rays of the sun, which gilded the dew-drops that hung upon leaf and blossom, and, while giving a brighter beauty to each rare flower, brought everything within the limits of ordinary experience. The young man rejoiced, that, in the heart of the barren city, he had the privilege of overlooking this spot of lovely and luxuriant vegetation. It would serve, he said to himself, as a symbolic language, to keep him in communion with Nature. Neither the sickly and thought-worn Doctor Giacomo Rappaccini, it is true, nor his brilliant daughter, were now visible; so that Giovanni could not determine how much of the singularity which he attributed to both, was due to their own qualities, and how much to his wonder-working fancy. But he was inclined to take a most rational view of the whole matter.

In the course of the day, he paid his respects to Signor Pietro Baglioni, Professor of Medicine in the University, a physician of eminent repute, to whom Giovanni had brought a letter of introduction. The Professor was an elderly personage, apparently of genial nature, and habits that might almost be called jovial; he kept the young man to dinner, and made himself very agreeable by the freedom and liveliness of his conversation, especially when warmed by a flask or two of Tuscan wine. Giovanni, conceiving that men of science, inhabitants of the same city, must needs be on familiar terms with one another, took an opportunity to mention the name of Doctor Rappaccini. But the Professor did not respond with so much cordiality as he had anticipated.

"Ill would it become a teacher of the divine art of medicine," said Professor Pietro Baglioni, in answer to a question of Giovanni, "to withhold due and well-considered praise of a physician so eminently skilled as Rappaccini. But, on the other hand, I should answer it but scantily to my conscience, were I to permit a worthy youth like yourself, Signor Giovanni, the son of an ancient friend, to imbibe erroneous ideas respecting a man who might hereafter chance to hold your life and death in his hands. The truth is, our worshipful Doctor Rappaccini has as much science as any member of the faculty—with perhaps one single exception—in Padua, or all Italy.

But there are certain grave objections to his professional character."

"And what are they?" asked the young man.

"Has my friend Giovanni any disease of body or heart, that he is so inquisitive about physicians?" said the Professor, with a smile. "But as for Rappaccini, it is said of him—and I, who know the man well, can answer for its truth—that he cares infinitely more for science than for mankind. His patients are interesting to him only as subjects for some new experiment. He would sacrifice human life, his own among the rest, or whatever else was dearest to him, for the sake of adding so much as a grain of mustard-seed to the great heap of his accumulated knowledge."

"Methinks he is an awful man, indeed," remarked Guasconti, mentally recalling the cold and purely intellectual aspect of Rappaccini. "And yet, worshipful Professor, is it not a noble spirit? Are there many men capable of so spiritual a love of science?"

"God forbid," answered the Professor, somewhat testily—"at least, unless they take sounder views of the healing art than those adopted by Rappaccini. It is his theory, that all medicinal virtues are comprised within those substances which we term vegetable poisons. These he cultivates with his own hands, and is said even to have produced new varieties of poison, more horribly deleterious than Nature, without the assistance of this learned person, would ever have plagued the world withal. That the Signor Doctor does less mischief than might be expected, with such dangerous substances, is undeniable. Now and then, it must be owned, he has effected—or seemed to effect—a marvellous cure. But, to tell you my private mind, Signor Giovanni, he should receive little credit for such instances of success—they being probably the work of chance—but should be held strictly accountable for his failures, which may justly be considered his own work."

The youth might have taken Baglioni's opinions with many grains of allowance, had he known that there was a professional warfare of long continuance between him and Doctor Rappaccini, in which the latter was generally thought to have gained the advantage. If the reader be inclined to judge for himself, we refer him to certain black-letter tracts on both sides, preserved in the medical department of the University of Padua.

"I know not, most learned Professor," returned Giovanni, after musing on what had been said of Rappaccini's exclusive zeal for science—"I know not how dearly this physician may love his art; but surely there is one object more dear to him. He has a daughter."

"Aha!" cried the Professor with a laugh. "So now our friend Giovanni's secret is out. You have heard of this daughter, whom all the young men in Padua are wild about, though not half a dozen have ever had the good hap to see her face. I know little of the Signora Beatrice, save that Rappaccini is said to have instructed her deeply in his science, and that, young and beautiful as fame reports her, she is already qualified to fill a professor's chair. Perchance her father destines her for mine! Other absurd rumors there be, not worth talking about, or listening to. So now, Signor Giovanni, drink off your glass of Lacryma."

Guasconti returned to his lodgings somewhat heated with the wine he had quaffed, and which caused his brain to swim with strange fantasies in reference to Doctor Rappaccini and the beautiful Beatrice. On his way, happening to pass by a florist's, he bought a fresh bouquet of flowers.

[Scene 3]

ASCENDING TO HIS CHAMBER, he seated himself near the window, but within the shadow thrown by the depth of the wall, so that he could look down into the garden with little risk of being discovered. All beneath his eye was a solitude. The strange plants were basking in the sunshine, and now and then nodding gently to one another, as if in acknowledgment of sympathy and kindred. In the midst, by the shattered fountain, grew the magnificent shrub, with its purple gems clustering all over it; they glowed in the air, and gleamed back again out of the depths of the pool, which thus seemed to overflow with colored radiance from the rich reflection that was steeped in it. At first, as we have said, the garden was a solitude. Soon, however,—as Giovanni had half hoped, half feared, would be the case,—a figure appeared beneath the antique sculptured portal, and came down between the rows of plants, inhaling their various perfumes, as if she were one of those beings of old classic fable, that lived upon sweet odors. On again beholding Beatrice, the young man was even startled to perceive how much her beauty exceeded his recollection of it; so brilliant, so vivid in its character, that she glowed amid the sunlight, and, as Giovanni whispered to himself, positively illuminated the more shadowy intervals of the garden path. Her face being now more revealed than on the former occasion, he was struck by its expression of simplicity and sweetness; qualities that had not entered into his idea of her character, and which made him ask anew, what manner of mortal she might be. Nor did he fail again to observe, or imagine, an analogy between the beautiful girl and the gorgeous shrub that hung its gem-like flowers over the fountain; a resemblance which Beatrice seemed to have indulged a fantastic humor in heightening, both by the arrangement of her dress and the selection of its hues.

Approaching the shrub, she threw open her arms, as with a passionate ardor, and drew its branches into an intimate embrace; so intimate, that her features were hidden in its leafy bosom, and her glistening ringlets all intermingled with the flowers.

"Give me thy breath, my sister," exclaimed Beatrice; "for I am faint with common air! And give me this flower of thine, which I separate with gentlest fingers from the stem, and place it close beside my heart."

With these words, the beautiful daughter of Rappaccini plucked one of the richest blossoms of the shrub, and was about to fasten it in her bosom. But now, unless Giovanni's draughts of wine had bewildered his senses, a singular incident occurred. A small orange colored reptile, of the lizard or chameleon species, chanced to be creeping along the path, just at the feet of Beatrice. It appeared to Giovanni—but, at the distance from which he gazed, he could scarcely have seen anything so minute—it appeared to him, however, that a drop or two of moisture from the broken stem of the flower descended upon the lizard's head. For an instant, the reptile contorted itself violently, and then lay motionless in the sunshine. Beatrice observed this remarkable phenomenon, and crossed herself, sadly, but without surprise; nor did she therefore hesitate to arrange the fatal flower in her bosom. There it blushed, and almost glimmered with the dazzling effect of a precious stone, adding to her dress and aspect the one appropriate charm, which nothing else in the world could have supplied. But Giovanni, out of the shadow of his window, bent forward and shrank back, and murmured and trembled.

"Am I awake? Have I my senses?" said he to himself. "What is this being?—beautiful, shall I call her?—or inexpressibly terrible?"

Beatrice now strayed carelessly through the garden, approaching closer beneath Giovanni's window, so that he was compelled to thrust his head quite out of its concealment, in order to gratify the intense and painful curiosity which she excited. At this moment, there came a beautiful insect over the garden wall; it had perhaps wandered through the city and found no flowers nor verdure among those antique haunts of men, until the heavy perfumes of Doctor Rappaccini's shrubs had lured it from afar. Without alighting on the flowers, this winged brightness seemed to be attracted by Beatrice, and lingered in the air and fluttered about her head. Now here it could not be but that Giovanni Guasconti's eyes deceived him. Be that as it might, he fancied that while Beatrice was gazing at the insect with childish delight, it grew faint and fell at her feet;—its bright wings shivered; it was dead—from no cause that he could discern, unless it were the atmosphere of her breath. Again Beatrice crossed herself and sighed heavily, as she bent over the dead insect.

An impulsive movement of Giovanni drew her eyes to the window. There she beheld the beautiful head of the young man—rather a Grecian than an Italian head, with fair, regular features, and a glistening of gold among his ringlets—gazing down upon her like a being that hovered in mid-air. Scarcely knowing what he did, Giovanni threw down the bouquet which he had hitherto held in his hand.

"Signora," said he, "there are pure and healthful flowers. Wear them for the sake of Giovanni Guasconti!"

"Thanks, Signor," replied Beatrice, with her rich voice that came forth as it were like a gush of music; and with a mirthful expression half childish and half woman-like. "I accept your gift, and would fain recompense it with this precious purple flower; but if I toss it into the air, it will not reach you. So Signor Guasconti must even content himself with my thanks."

She lifted the bouquet from the ground, and then as if inwardly ashamed at having stepped aside from her maidenly reserve to respond to a stranger's greeting, passed swiftly homeward through the garden. But, few as the moments were, it seemed to Giovanni when she was on the point of vanishing beneath the sculptured portal, that his beautiful bouquet was already beginning to wither in her grasp. It was an idle thought; there could be no possibility of distinguishing a faded flower from a fresh one, at so great a distance.

[Scene 4]

FOR MANY DAYS AFTER THIS INCIDENT, the young man avoided the window that looked into Doctor Rappaccini's garden, as if something ugly and monstrous would have blasted his eye-sight, had he been betrayed into a glance. He felt conscious of having put himself, to a certain extent, within the influence of an unintelligible power, by the communication which he had opened with Beatrice. The wisest course would have been, if his heart were in any real danger, to quit his lodgings and Padua itself, at once; the next wiser, to have accustomed himself, as far as possible, to the familiar and day-light view of Beatrice; thus bringing her rigidly and systematically within the limits of ordinary experience. Least of all, while avoiding her sight, should Giovanni have remained so near this extraordinary being, that the proximity and possibility even of intercourse, should give a kind of substance and reality to the wild vagaries which his imagination ran riot continually in producing. Guasconti had not a deep heart—or at all events, its depths were not sounded now—but he had a quick fancy, and an ardent southern temperament, which rose every instant to a higher fever-pitch. Whether or no Beatrice possessed those terrible attributes—that fatal breath—the affinity with those so beautiful and deadly flowers—which were indicated by what Giovanni had witnessed, she had at least instilled a fierce and subtle poison into his system. It was not love, although her rich beauty was a madness to him; nor horror, even while he fancied her spirit to be imbued with the same baneful essence that seemed to pervade her physical frame; but a wild offspring of both love and horror that had each parent in it, and burned like one and shivered like the other. Giovanni knew not what to dread; still less did he know what to hope; yet hope and dread kept a continual warfare in his breast, alternately vanquishing one another and starting up afresh to renew the contest. Blessed are all simple emotions, be they dark or bright! It is the lurid intermixture of the two that produces the illuminating blaze of the infernal regions.

Sometimes he endeavored to assuage the fever of his spirit by a rapid walk through the streets of Padua, or beyond its gates; his footsteps kept time with the throbbings of his brain, so that the walk was apt to accelerate itself to a race. One day, he found himself arrested; his arm was seized by a portly personage who had turned back on recognizing the young man, and expended much breath in overtaking him.

"Signor Giovanni!—stay, my young friend!" —cried he. "Have you forgotten me? That might well be the case, if I were as much altered as yourself."

It was Baglioni, whom Giovanni had avoided, ever since their first meeting, from a doubt that the Professor's sagacity would look too deeply into his secrets. Endeavoring to recover himself, he stared forth wildly from his inner world into the outer one, and spoke like a man in a dream.

"Yes; I am Giovanni Guasconti. You are Professor Pietro Baglioni. Now let me pass!"

"Not yet—not yet, Signor Giovanni Guasconti," said the Professor, smiling, but at the same time scrutinizing the youth with an earnest glance. "What, did I grow up side by side with your father, and shall his son pass me like a stranger, in these old streets of Padua? Stand still, Signor

Giovanni; for we must have a word or two before we part."

"Speedily, then, most worshipful Professor, speedily!" said Giovanni, with feverish impatience. "Does not your worship see that I am in haste?"

Now, while he was speaking, there came a man in black along the street, stooping and moving feebly, like a person in inferior health. His face was all overspread with a most sickly and sallow hue, but yet so pervaded with an expression of piercing and active intellect, that an observer might easily have overlooked the merely physical attributes, and have seen only this wonderful energy. As he passed, this person exchanged a cold and distant salutation with Baglioni, but fixed his eyes upon Giovanni with an intentness that seemed to bring out whatever was within him worthy of notice. Nevertheless, there was a peculiar quietness in the look, as if taking merely a speculative, not a human interest, in the young man.

"It is Doctor Rappaccini!" whispered the Professor, when the stranger had passed.—"Has he ever seen your face before?"

"Not that I know," answered Giovanni, starting at the name.

"He *has* seen you!—he must have seen you!" said Baglioni, hastily. "For some purpose or other, this man of science is making a study of you. I know that look of his! It is the same that coldly illuminates his face, as he bends over a bird, a mouse, or a butterfly, which, in pursuance of some experiment, he has killed by the perfume of a flower;—a look as deep as Nature itself, but without Nature's warmth of love. Signor Giovanni, I will stake my life upon it, you are the subject of one of Rappaccini's experiments!"

"Will you make a fool of me?" cried Giovanni, passionately. "*That,* Signor Professor, were an untoward experiment."

"Patience, patience!" replied the imperturbable Professor. "I tell thee, my poor Giovanni, that Rappaccini has a scientific interest in thee. Thou hast fallen into fearful hands! And the Signora Beatrice? What part does she act in this mystery?"

But Guasconti, finding Baglioni's pertinacity intolerable, here broke away, and was gone before the Professor could again seize his arm. He looked after the young man intently, and shook his head.

"This must not be," said Baglioni to himself. "The youth is the son of my old friend, and shall not come to any harm from which the arcana of medical science can preserve him. Besides, it is too insufferable an impertinence in Rappaccini thus to snatch the lad out of my own hands, as I may say, and make use of him for his infernal experiments. This daughter of his! It shall be looked to. Perchance, most learned Rappaccini, I may foil you where you little dream of it!"

[Scene 5]

MEANWHILE, GIOVANNI HAD PURSUED a circuitous route, and at length found himself at the door of his lodgings. As he crossed the threshold, he was met by old Lisabetta, who smirked and smiled, and was evidently desirous to attract his attention; vainly, however, as the ebullition of his feelings had momentarily subsided into a cold and dull vacuity. He turned his eyes full upon the withered face that was puckering itself into a smile, but seemed to behold it not. The old dame, therefore, laid her grasp upon his cloak.

"Signor!—Signor!" whispered she, still with a smile over the whole breadth of her visage, so that it looked not unlike a grotesque carving in wood, darkened by centuries—"Listen, Signor! There is a private entrance into the garden!"

"What do you say?" exclaimed Giovanni, turning quickly about, as if an inanimate thing should start into feverish life.—"A private entrance into Doctor Rappaccini's garden!"

"Hush! hush!—not so loud!" whispered Lisabetta, putting her hand over his mouth. "Yes; into the worshipful Doctor's garden, where you may see all his fine shrubbery. Many a young man in Padua would give gold to be admitted among those flowers."

Giovanni put a piece of gold into her hand.

"Show me the way," said he.

A surmise, probably excited by his conversation with Baglioni, crossed his mind, that this interposition of old Lisabetta might perchance be connected with the intrigue, whatever were its nature, in which the Professor seemed to suppose that Doctor Rappaccini was involving him. But such a suspicion, though it disturbed Giovanni, was inadequate to restrain him. The instant he was aware of the possibility of approaching Beatrice, it seemed an absolute necessity of his existence to do so. It mattered not whether she were angel or demon; he was irrevocably within her sphere, and must obey the law that whirled him onward, in ever lessening circles, towards a result which he did not attempt to foreshadow. And yet, strange to say, there came across him a sudden doubt, whether this intense interest on his part were not delusory—whether it were really of so deep and positive a nature as to justify him in now thrusting himself into an incalculable position—whether it were not merely the fantasy of a young man's brain, only slightly, or not at all, connected with his heart!

He paused—hesitated—turned half about—but again went on. His withered guide led him along several obscure passages, and finally undid a door, through which, as it was opened, there came the sight and sound of rustling leaves, with the broken sunshine glimmering among them. Giovanni stepped forth, and forcing himself through the entanglement of a shrub that wreathed its tendrils over the hidden entrance, he stood beneath his own window, in the open area of Doctor Rappaccini's garden.

How often is it the case, that, when impossibilities have come to pass, and dreams have condensed their misty substance into tangible realities, we find ourselves calm, and even coldly self-possessed, amid circumstances which it would have been a delirium of joy or agony to anticipate! Fate delights to thwart us thus. Passion will choose his own time to rush upon the scene, and lingers sluggishly behind, when an appropriate adjustment of events would seem to summon his appearance. So was it now with Giovanni. Day after day, his pulses had throbbed with feverish blood, at the improbable idea of an interview with Beatrice, and of standing with her, face to face, in this very garden, basking in the oriental sunshine of her beauty, and snatching from her full gaze the mystery which he deemed the riddle of his own existence. But now there was a singular and untimely equanimity within his breast. He threw a glance around the garden to discover if Beatrice or her father were present, and perceiving that he was alone, began a critical observation of the plants.

The aspect of one and all of them dissatisfied him; their gorgeousness seemed fierce, passionate, and even unnatural. There was hardly an individual shrub which a wanderer, straying by himself through a forest, would not have been startled to find growing wild, as if an unearthly face had glared at him out of the thicket. Several, also, would have shocked a delicate instinct by an appearance of artificialness, indicating that there had been such commixture, and, as it were, adultery of various vegetable species, that the production was no longer of God's making, but the monstrous offspring of man's depraved fancy, glowing with only an evil mockery of beauty. They were probably the result of experiment, which, in one or two cases, had succeeded in mingling plants individually lovely into a compound possessing the questionable and ominous character that distinguished the whole growth of the garden. In fine, Giovanni recognized but two or three plants in the collection, and those of a kind that he well knew to be poisonous. While busy with these contemplations, he heard the rustling of a silken garment, and turning, beheld Beatrice emerging from beneath the sculptured portal.

Giovanni had not considered with himself what should be his deportment; whether he should apologize for his intrusion into the garden, or assume that he was there with the privity, at least, if not by the desire, of Doctor Rappaccini or his daughter. But Beatrice's manner placed him at his ease, though leaving him still in doubt by what agency he had gained admittance. She came lightly along the path, and met him near the broken fountain. There was surprise in her face, but brightened by a simple and kind expression of pleasure.

"You are a connoisseur in flowers, Signor," said Beatrice with a smile, alluding to the bouquet which he had flung her from the window. "It is no marvel, therefore, if the sight of my father's rare collection has tempted you to take a nearer view. If he were here, he could tell you many strange and interesting facts as to the nature and habits of these shrubs, for he has spent a lifetime in such studies, and this garden is his world."

"And yourself, lady"—observed Giovanni—"if fame says true—you, likewise, are deeply skilled in the virtues indicated by these rich blossoms, and these spicy perfumes. Would you deign to be my instructress, I should prove an apter scholar than under Signor Rappaccini himself."

"Are there such idle rumors?" asked Beatrice, with the music of a pleasant laugh. "Do people say that I am skilled in my father's science of plants? What a jest is there! No; though I have grown up among these flowers, I know no more of them than their hues and perfume; and sometimes, methinks I would fain rid myself of even that small knowledge. There are many flowers here, and those not the least brilliant, that shock and offend me, when they meet my eye. But, pray, Signor, do not believe these stories about my science. Believe nothing of me save what you see with your own eyes."

"And must I believe all that I have seen with my own eyes?" asked Giovanni pointedly, while the recollection of former scenes made him shrink. "No, Signora, you demand too little of me. Bid me believe nothing, save what comes from your own lips."

It would appear that Beatrice understood him. There came a deep flush to her cheek; but she looked full into Giovanni's eyes, and responded to his gaze of uneasy suspicion with a queen-like haughtiness.

"I do so bid you, Signor!" she replied. "Forget whatever you may have fancied in regard to me. If true to the outward senses, still it may be false in its essence. But the words of Beatrice Rappaccini's lips are true from the heart outward. Those you may believe!"

A fervor glowed in her whole aspect, and beamed upon Giovanni's consciousness like the light of truth itself. But while she spoke, there was a fragrance in the atmosphere around her rich and delightful, though evanescent, yet which the young man, from an indefinable reluctance, scarcely dared to draw into his lungs. It might be the odor of the flowers. Could it be Beatrice's breath, which thus embalmed her words with a strange richness, as if by steeping them in her heart? A faintness passed like a shadow over Giovanni, and flitted away; he seemed to gaze through the beautiful girl's eyes into her transparent soul, and felt no more doubt or fear.

The tinge of passion that had colored Beatrice's manner vanished; she became gay, and appeared to derive a pure delight from her communion with the youth, not unlike what the maiden of a lonely island might have felt, conversing with a voyager from the civilized world. Evidently her experience of life had been confined within the limits of that garden. She talked now about matters as simple as the day-light or summer-clouds, and now asked questions in reference to the city, or Giovanni's distant home, his friends, his mother, and his sisters; questions indicating such seclusion, and such lack of familiarity with modes and forms, that Giovanni responded as if to an infant. Her spirit gushed out before him like a fresh rill, that was just catching its first glimpse of the sunlight, and wondering, at the reflections of earth and sky which were flung into its bosom. There came thoughts, too, from a deep source, and fantasies of a gem-like brilliancy, as if diamonds and rubies sparkled upward among the bubbles of the fountain. Ever and anon, there gleamed across the young man's mind a sense of wonder, that he should be walking side by side with the being who had so wrought upon his imagination—whom he had idealized in such hues of terror—in whom he had positively witnessed such manifestations of dreadful attributes—that he should be conversing with Beatrice like a brother, and should find her so human and so maiden-like. But such reflections were only momentary; the effect of her character was too real, not to make itself familiar at once.

In this free intercourse, they had strayed through the garden, and now, after many turns among its avenues, were come to the shattered fountain, beside which grew the magnificent shrub with its treasury of glowing blossoms. A fragrance was diffused from it, which Giovanni recognized as identical with that which he had attributed to Beatrice's breath, but incomparably more powerful. As her eyes fell upon it, Giovanni beheld her press her hand to her bosom, as if her heart were throbbing suddenly and painfully.

"For the first time in my life," murmured she, addressing the shrub, "I had forgotten thee!"

"I remember, Signora," said Giovanni, "that you once promised to reward me with one of these living gems for the bouquet, which I had the happy boldness to fling to your feet. Permit me now to pluck it as a memorial of this interview."

He made a step towards the shrub, with extended hand. But Beatrice darted forward, uttering a shriek that went through his heart like a dagger. She caught his hand, and drew it back with the whole force of her slender figure. Giovanni felt her touch thrilling through his fibres.

"Touch it not!" exclaimed she, in a voice of agony. "Not for thy life! It is fatal!"

Then, hiding her face, she fled from him, and vanished beneath the sculptured portal. As Giovanni followed her with his eyes, he beheld the emaciated figure and pale intelligence of Doctor Rappaccini, who had been watching the scene, he knew not how long, within the shadow of the entrance.

[Scene 6]

NO SOONER WAS GUASCONTI ALONE in his chamber, than the image of Beatrice came back to his passionate musings, invested with all the witchery that had been gathering around it ever since his first glimpse of her, and now likewise imbued with a tender warmth of girlish womanhood. She was human: her nature was endowed with all gentle and feminine qualities; she was worthiest to be worshipped; she was capable, surely, on her part, of the height and heroism of love. Those tokens, which he had hitherto considered as proofs of a frightful peculiarity in her physical and moral system, were now either forgotten, or, by the subtle sophistry of passion, transmuted into a golden crown of enchantment, rendering Beatrice the more admirable, by so much as she was the more unique. Whatever had looked ugly, was now beautiful; or, if incapable of such a change, it stole away and hid itself among those shapeless half-ideas, which throng the dim region beyond the daylight of our perfect consciousness. Thus did Giovanni spend the night, nor fell asleep, until the dawn had begun to awake the slumbering flowers in Doctor Rappaccini's garden, whither his dreams doubtless led him. Up rose the sun in his due season, and flinging his beams upon the young man's eyelids, awoke him to a sense of pain. When thoroughly aroused, he became sensible of a burning and tingling agony in his hand—in his right hand—the very hand which Beatrice had grasped in her own, when he was on the point of plucking one of the gem-like flowers. On the back of that hand there was now a purple print, like that of four small fingers, and the likeness of a slender thumb upon his wrist.

Oh, how stubbornly does love—or even that cunning semblance of love which flourishes in the imagination, but strikes no depth of root into the heart—how stubbornly does it hold its faith, until the moment come, when it is doomed to vanish into thin mist! Giovanni wrapt a handkerchief about his hand, and wondered what evil thing had stung him, and soon forgot his pain in a reverie of Beatrice.

After the first interview, a second was in the inevitable course of what we call fate. A third; a fourth; and a meeting with Beatrice in the garden was no longer an incident in Giovanni's daily life, but the whole space in which he might be said to live; for the anticipation and memory of that ecstatic hour made up the remainder. Nor was it otherwise with the daughter of Rappaccini. She watched for the youth's appearance, and flew to his side with confidence as unreserved as if they had been playmates from early infancy—as if they were such playmates still. If, by any unwonted chance, he failed to come at the appointed moment, she stood beneath the window, and sent up the rich sweetness of her tones to float around him in his chamber, and echo and reverberate throughout his heart—"Giovanni! Giovanni! Why tarriest thou? Come down!" And down he hastened into that Eden of poisonous flowers.

But, with all this intimate familiarity, there was still a reserve in Beatrice's demeanor, so rigidly and invariably sustained, that the idea of infringing it scarcely occurred to his imagination. By all appreciable signs, they loved; they had looked love, with eyes that conveyed the holy secret from the depths of one soul into the depths of the other, as if it were too sacred to be whispered by the way; they had even spoken love, in those gushes of passion when their spirits darted forth in articulated breath, like tongues of long-hidden flame; and yet there had been no seal of lips, no clasp of hands, nor any slightest caress, such as love claims and hallows. He had never touched one of the gleaming ringlets of her hair; her garment—so marked was the physical barrier between them—had never been waved against him by a breeze. On the few occasions when Giovanni had seemed tempted to overstep the limit, Beatrice grew so sad, so stern, and withal wore such a look of desolate separation, shuddering at itself, that not a spoken word was requisite to repel him. At such times, he was startled at the horrible suspicions that rose, monster-like, out of the caverns of his heart, and stared him in the face; his love grew thin and faint as the morning-mist; his doubts alone had substance. But when Beatrice's face brightened again, after the momentary shadow, she was transformed at once from the mysterious, questionable being, whom he had watched with so much awe and horror; she was now the beautiful and unsophisticated girl, whom he felt that his spirit knew with a certainty beyond all other knowledge.

A considerable time had now passed since Giovanni's last meeting with Baglioni. One morning, however, he was disagreeably surprised by a visit from the Professor, whom he had scarcely thought of for whole weeks, and would willingly have forgotten still longer. Given up, as he had long been, to a pervading excitement, he could tolerate no companions, except upon condition of their perfect sympathy with his present state of feeling. Such sympathy was not to be expected from Professor Baglioni.

The visitor chatted carelessly, for a few moments, about the gossip of the city and the University, and then took up another topic.

"I have been reading an old classic author lately," said he, "and met with a story that strangely interested me. Possibly you may remember it. It is of an Indian prince, who sent a beautiful woman as a present to Alexander the Great. She was as lovely as the dawn, and gorgeous as the sunset; but what especially distinguished her was a certain rich perfume in her breath—richer than a garden of Persian roses. Alexander, as was natural to a youthful conqueror, fell in love at first sight with this magnificent stranger. But a certain sage physician, happening to be present, discovered a terrible secret in regard to her."

"And what was that?" asked Giovanni, turning his eyes downward to avoid those of the Professor.

"That this lovely woman," continued Baglioni, with emphasis, "had been nourished with poisons from her birth upward, until her whole nature was so imbued with them, that she herself had become the deadliest poison in existence. Poison was her element of life. With that rich perfume of her breath, she blasted the very air. Her love would have been poison!—her embrace death! Is not this a marvellous tale?"

"A childish fable," answered Giovanni, nervously starting from his chair. "I marvel how your worship finds time to read such nonsense, among your graver studies."

"By the bye," said the Professor, looking uneasily about him, "what singular fragrance is this in your apartment? Is it the perfume of your gloves? It is faint, but delicious, and yet, after all, by no means agreeable. Were I to breathe it long, methinks it would make me ill. It is like the breath of a flower—but I see no flowers in the chamber."

"Nor are there any," replied Giovanni, who had turned pale as the Professor spoke; "nor, I think, is there any fragrance, except in your worship's imagination. Odors, being a sort of element combined of the sensual and the spiritual, are apt to deceive us in this manner. The recollection of a perfume—the bare idea of it—may easily be mistaken for a present reality."

"Aye; but my sober imagination does not often play such tricks," said Baglioni; "and were I to fancy any kind of odor, it would be that of some vile apothecary drug, wherewith my fingers are likely enough to be imbued. Our worshipful friend Rappaccini, as I have heard, tinctures his medicaments with odors richer than those of Araby. Doubtless, likewise, the fair and learned Signora Beatrice would minister to her patients with draughts as sweet as a maiden's breath. But wo to him that sips them!"

Giovanni's face evinced many contending emotions. The tone in which the Professor alluded to the pure and lovely daughter of Rappaccini was a torture to his soul; and yet, the intimation of a view of her character, opposite to his own, gave instantaneous distinctness to a thousand dim suspicions, which now grinned at him like so many demons. But he strove hard to quell them, and to respond to Baglioni with a true lover's perfect faith.

"Signor Professor," said he, "you were my father's friend—perchance, too, it is your purpose to act a friendly part towards his son. I would fain feel nothing towards you save respect and deference. But I pray you to observe, Signor, that there is one subject on which we must not speak. You know not the Signora Beatrice. You cannot, therefore, estimate the wrong—the blasphemy, I may even say—that is offered to her character by a light or injurious word."

"Giovanni!—my poor Giovanni!" answered the Professor, with a calm expression of pity, "I know this wretched girl far better than yourself. You shall hear the truth in respect to the poisoner Rappaccini, and his poisonous daughter. Yes; poisonous as she is beautiful! Listen; for even should you do violence to my gray hairs, it shall not silence me. That old fable of the Indian woman has become a truth, by the deep and deadly science of Rappaccini, and in the person of the lovely Beatrice!"

Giovanni groaned and hid his face.

"Her father," continued Baglioni, "was not restrained by natural affection from offering up his child, in this horrible manner, as the victim of his insane zeal for science. For—let us do him justice—he is as true a man of science as ever distilled his own heart in an alembic. What, then, will be your fate? Beyond a doubt, you are selected as the material of some new experiment. Perhaps the result is to be death—perhaps a fate more awful still! Rappaccini, with what he calls the interest of science before his eyes, will hesitate at nothing."

"It is a dream!" muttered Giovanni to himself, "surely it is a dream!"

"But," resumed the Professor, "be of good cheer, son of my friend! It is not yet too late for the rescue. Possibly, we may even succeed in bringing back this miserable child within the limits of ordinary nature, from which her father's madness has estranged her. Behold this little silver vase! It was wrought by the hands of the renowned Benvenuto Cellini, and is well worthy to be a love-gift to the fairest dame in Italy. But its contents are invaluable. One little sip of this antidote would have rendered the most virulent poisons of the Borgias innocuous. Doubt not that it will be as efficacious against those of Rappaccini. Bestow the vase, and the precious liquid within it, on your Beatrice, and hopefully await the result."

Baglioni laid a small, exquisitely wrought silver phial on the table, and withdrew, leaving what he had said to produce its effect upon the young man's mind.

"We will thwart Rappaccini yet!" thought he, chuckling to himself, as he descended the stairs. "But, let us confess the truth of him, he is a wonderful man!—a wonderful man indeed! A vile empiric, however, in his practice, and therefore not to be tolerated by those who respect the good old rules of the medical profession!"

[Scene 7]

THROUGHOUT GIOVANNI'S WHOLE ACQUAINTANCE with Beatrice, he had occasionally, as we have said, been haunted by dark surmises as to her character. Yet, so thoroughly had she made herself felt by him as a simple, natural, most affectionate and guileless creature, that the image now held up by Professor Baglioni, looked as strange and incredible, as if it were not in accordance with his own original conception. True, there were ugly recollections connected with his first glimpses of the beautiful girl; he could not quite forget the bouquet that withered in her grasp, and the insect that perished amid the sunny air, by no ostensible agency save the fragrance of her breath. These incidents, however, dissolving in the pure light of her character, had no longer the efficacy of facts, but were acknowledged as mistaken fantasies, by whatever testimony of the senses they might appear to be substantiated. There is something truer and more real, than what we can see with the eyes, and touch with the finger. On such better evidence, had Giovanni founded his confidence in Beatrice, though rather by the necessary force of her high attributes, than by any deep and generous faith on his part. But, now, his spirit was incapable of sustaining itself at the height to which the early enthusiasm of passion had exalted it; he fell down, grovelling among earthly doubts, and defiled therewith the pure whiteness of Beatrice's image. Not that he gave her up; he did but distrust. He resolved to institute some decisive test that should satisfy him, once for all, whether there were those dreadful peculiarities in her physical nature, which could not be supposed to exist without some corresponding monstrosity of soul. His eyes, gazing down afar, might have deceived him as to the lizard, the insect, and the flowers. But if he could witness, at the distance of a few paces, the sudden blight of one fresh and healthful flower in Beatrice's hand, there would be room for no further question. With this idea, he hastened to the florist's, and purchased a bouquet that was still gemmed with the morning dew-drops.

It was now the customary hour of his daily interview with Beatrice. Before descending into the garden, Giovanni failed not to look at his figure in the mirror; a vanity to be expected in a beautiful young man, yet, as displaying itself at that troubled and feverish moment, the token of a certain shallowness of feeling and insincerity of character. He did gaze, however, and said to himself, that his features had never before possessed so rich a grace, nor his eyes such vivacity, nor his cheeks so warm a hue of superabundant life.

"At least," thought he, "her poison has not yet insinuated itself into my system. I am no flower to perish in her grasp!"

With that thought, he turned his eyes on the bouquet, which he had never once laid aside from his hand. A thrill of indefinable horror shot through his frame, on perceiving that those dewy flowers were already beginning to droop; they wore the aspect of things that had been fresh and lovely, yesterday. Giovanni grew white as marble, and stood motionless before the mirror, staring at his own reflection there, as at the likeness of something frightful. He remembered Baglioni's remark about the fragrance that seemed to pervade the chamber. It must have been the poison in his breath! Then he shuddered—shuddered at himself! Recovering from his stupor, he began to watch, with curious eye, a spider that was busily at work, hanging its web from the antique cornice of the apartment, crossing and re-crossing the artful system of interwoven lines, as vigorous and active a spider as ever dangled from an old ceiling. Giovanni bent towards the insect, and emitted a deep, long breath. The spider suddenly ceased its toil; the web vibrated with a tremor originating in the body of the small artizan. Again Giovanni sent forth a breath, deeper, longer, and imbued with a venomous feeling out of his heart; he knew not whether he were wicked or only desperate. The spider made a convulsive gripe with his limbs, and hung dead across the window.

"Accursed! Accursed!" muttered Giovanni, addressing himself. "Hast thou grown so poisonous, that this deadly insect perishes by thy breath?"

At that moment, a rich, sweet voice came floating up from the garden: "Giovanni! Giovanni! It is past the hour! Why tarriest thou! Come down!"

"Yes," muttered Giovanni again. "She is the only being whom my breath may not slay! Would that it might!"

He rushed down, and in an instant, was standing before the bright and loving eyes of Beatrice. A moment ago, his wrath and despair had been so fierce that he could have desired nothing so much as to wither her by a glance. But, with her actual presence, there came influences which had too real an existence to be at once shaken off; recollections of the delicate and benign power of her feminine nature, which had so often enveloped him in a religious calm; recollections of many a holy and passionate outgush of her heart, when the pure fountain had been unsealed from its depths, and made visible in its transparency to his mental eye; recollections which, had Giovanni known how to estimate them, would have assured him that all this ugly mystery was but an earthly illusion, and that, whatever mist of evil might seem to have gathered over her, the real Beatrice was a heavenly angel. Incapable as he was of such high faith, still her presence had not utterly lost its magic. Giovanni's rage was quelled into an aspect of sullen insensibility. Beatrice, with a quick spiritual sense, immediately felt that there was a gulf of blackness between them, which neither he nor she could pass. They walked on together, sad and silent, and came thus to the marble fountain, and to its pool of water on the ground, in the midst of which grew the shrub that bore gem-like blossoms. Giovanni was affrighted at the eager enjoyment—the appetite, as it were—with which he found himself inhaling the fragrance of the flowers.

"Beatrice," asked he abruptly, "whence came this shrub!"

"My father created it," answered she, with simplicity.

"Created it! created it!" repeated Giovanni. "What mean you, Beatrice?"

"He is a man fearfully acquainted with the secrets of nature," replied Beatrice; "and, at the hour when I first drew breath, this plant sprang from the soil, the offspring of his science, of his intellect, while I was but his earthly child. Approach it not!" continued she, observing with terror that Giovanni was drawing nearer to the shrub. "It has qualities that you little dream of. But I, dearest Giovanni—I grew up and blossomed with the plant, and was nourished with its breath. It was my sister, and I loved it with a human affection: for—alas! hast thou not suspected it? there was an awful doom."

Here Giovanni frowned so darkly upon her that Beatrice paused and trembled. But her faith in his tenderness reassured her, and made her blush that she had doubted for an instant.

"There was an awful doom," she continued,—"the effect of my father's fatal love of science—

which estranged me from all society of my kind. Until Heaven sent thee, dearest Giovanni, Oh! how lonely was thy poor Beatrice!"

"Was it a hard doom?" asked Giovanni, fixing his eyes upon her.

"Only of late have I known how hard it was," answered she tenderly. "Oh, yes; but my heart was torpid, and therefore quiet."

Giovanni's rage broke forth from his sullen gloom like a lightning-flash out of a dark cloud.

"Accursed one!" cried he, with venomous scorn and anger. "And finding thy solitude wearisome, thou hast severed me, likewise, from all the warmth of life, and enticed me into thy region of unspeakable horror!"

"Giovanni!" exclaimed Beatrice, turning her large bright eyes upon his face. The force of his words had not found its way into her mind; she was merely thunder-struck.

"Yes, poisonous thing!" repeated Giovanni, beside himself with passion. "Thou hast done it! Thou hast blasted me! Thou hast filled my veins with poison! Thou hast made me as hateful, as ugly, as loathsome and deadly a creature as thyself—a world's wonder of hideous monstrosity! Now—if our breath be happily as fatal to ourselves as to all others—let us join our lips in one kiss of unutterable hatred, and so die!"

"What has befallen me?" murmured Beatrice, with a low moan out of her heart. "Holy Virgin pity me, a poor heartbroken child!"

"Thou! Dost thou pray?" cried Giovanni, still with the same fiendish scorn. "Thy very prayers, as they come from thy lips, taint the atmosphere with death. Yes, yes; let us pray! Let us to church, and dip our fingers in the holy water at the portal! They that come after us will perish as by a pestilence. Let us sign crosses in the air! It will be scattering curses abroad in the likeness of holy symbols!"

"Giovanni," said Beatrice calmly, for her grief was beyond passion, "Why dost thou join thyself with me thus in those terrible words? I, it is true, am the horrible thing thou namest me. But thou!—what hast thou to do, save with one other shudder at my hideous misery, to go forth out of the garden and mingle with thy race, and forget that there ever crawled on earth such a monster as poor Beatrice?"

"Dost thou pretend ignorance?" asked Giovanni, scowling upon her. "Behold! This power have I gained from the pure daughter of Rappaccini!"

There was a swarm of summer-insects flitting through the air, in search of the food promised by the flower-odors of the fatal garden. They circled round Giovanni's head, and were evidently attracted towards him by the same influence which had drawn them, for an instant, within the sphere of several of the shrubs. He sent forth a breath among them, and smiled bitterly at Beatrice, as at least a score of the insects fell dead upon the ground.

"I see it! I see it!" shrieked Beatrice. "It is my father's fatal science? No, no, Giovanni, it was not I! Never, never! I dreamed only to love thee, and be with thee a little time, and so to let thee pass away, leaving but thine image in mine heart. For, Giovanni—believe it—though my body be nourished with poison, my spirit is God's creature, and craves love as its daily food. But my father!—he has united us in this fearful sympathy. Yes; spurn me!—tread upon me!—kill me! Oh, what is death, after such words as thine? But it was not I! Not for a world of bliss would I have done it!"

Giovanni's passion had exhausted itself in its outburst from his lips. There now came across him a sense, mournful, and not without tenderness, of the intimate and peculiar relationship between Beatrice and himself. They stood, as it were, in an utter solitude, which would be made none the less solitary by the densest throng of human life. Ought not, then, the desert of humanity around them to press this insulated pair closer together? If they should be cruel to one another, who was there to be kind to them? Besides, thought Giovanni, might there not still be a hope of his returning within the limits of ordinary nature, and leading Beatrice—the redeemed Beatrice—by the hand? Oh, weak, and selfish, and unworthy spirit, that could dream of an earthly union and earthly happiness as possible, after such deep love had been so bitterly wronged as was Beatrice's love by Giovanni's blighting words! No, no; there could be no such hope. She must pass heavily, with that broken heart, across the borders of Time—she must bathe her hurts in some fount of Paradise, and forget her grief in the light of immortality—and *there* be well!

But Giovanni did not know it.

"Dear Beatrice," said he, approaching her, while she shrank away, as always at his approach, but now with a different impulse—"dearest Beatrice, our fate is not yet so desperate. Behold! There is a medicine, potent, as a wise physician has assured me, and almost divine in its efficacy. It is composed of ingredients the most opposite to those by which thy awful father has brought this calamity upon thee and me. It is distilled of blessed herbs. Shall we not quaff it together, and thus be purified from evil?"

"Give it me!" said Beatrice, extending her hand to receive the little silver phial which Giovanni took from his bosom. She added, with a peculiar emphasis: "I will drink—but do thou await the result."

She put Baglioni's antidote to her lips; and, at the same moment, the figure of Rappaccini emerged from the portal, and came slowly towards the marble fountain. As he drew near, the pale man of science seemed to gaze with a triumphant expression at the beautiful youth and maiden, as might an artist who should spend his life in achieving a picture or a group of statuary, and finally be satisfied with his success. He paused—his bent form grew erect with conscious power, he spread out his hand over them, in the attitude of a father imploring a blessing upon his children. But those were the same hands that had thrown poison into the stream of their lives! Giovanni trembled. Beatrice shuddered very nervously, and pressed her hand upon her heart.

"My daughter," said Rappaccini, "thou art no longer lonely in the world! Pluck one of those precious gems from thy sister shrub, and bid thy bridegroom wear it in his bosom. It will not harm him now! My science, and the sympathy between thee and him, have so wrought within his system, that he now stands apart from common men, as thou dost, daughter of my pride and triumph, from ordinary women. Pass on, then, through the world, most dear to one another, and dreadful to all besides!"

"My father," said Beatrice, feebly—and still, as she spoke, she kept her hand upon her heart—"wherefore didst thou inflict this miserable doom upon thy child?"

"Miserable!" exclaimed Rappaccini. "What mean you, foolish girl? Dost thou deem it misery to be endowed with marvellous gifts, against which no power nor strength could avail an enemy? Misery, to be able to quell the mightiest with a breath? Misery, to be as terrible as thou art beautiful? Wouldst thou, then, have preferred the condition of a weak woman, exposed to all evil, and capable of none?"

"I would fain have been loved, not feared," murmured Beatrice, sinking down upon the ground.—"But now it matters not; I am going, father, where the evil, which thou hast striven to mingle with my being, will pass away like a dream—like the fragrance of these poisonous flowers, which will no longer taint my breath among the flowers of Eden. Farewell, Giovanni! Thy words of hatred are like lead within my heart—but they, too, will fall away as I ascend. Oh, was there not, from the first, more poison in thy nature than in mine?"

To Beatrice—so radically had her earthly part been wrought upon by Rappaccini's skill—as poison had been life, so the powerful antidote was death. And thus the poor victim of man's ingenuity and of thwarted nature, and of the fatality that attends all such efforts of perverted wisdom, perished there, at the feet of her father and Giovanni. Just at that moment, Professor Pietro Baglioni looked forth from the window, and called loudly, in a tone of triumph mixed with horror, to the thunder-stricken man of science: "Rappaccini! Rappaccini! And is *this* the upshot of your experiment?"

THE END

Readers Theater Script, Secondary Level

Readers Theater Adaptation of
Hawthorne's "Rappaccini's Daughter"
By Sharon Adelman Reyes

Characters
Doctor Giacomo Rappaccini, a scientist specializing in botany
Beatrice Rappaccini, his daughter
Lisabetta, a housekeeper
Giovanni Guasconti, a student
Professor Pietro Baglioni, of the University of Padua
Narrator One (opens and closes each scene)
Narrator Two (relays action relating to Giovanni)
Narrator Three (relays action relating to Beatrice)
Narrator Four (relays action relating to Baglioni)

Pronunciation Key
Doctor Giacomo Rappaccini: JAHK uh mo rahp uh CHEE nee
Giovanni Guasconti: joh VAH nee gwa SKOHN tee
Beatrice Rappaccini: bay ah TREE chay rahp uh CHEE nee
Professor Pietro Baglioni: PYET ro bal YOH nee
Lisabetta: leez uh BET uh
Padua: PAH dwah
Signor: see NYOR
Signora: see NYOR uh

Tech Crew
Lights: Dim at beginning and end of production and between scenes
Music: Play at beginning and end of production and between scenes
Projection: Use PowerPoint slides as backdrops for each scene
Aroma: Spray essential oil formula into the air before Scenes 5 & 7
Ushers: As needed

Props and Costume Pieces

Doctor Giacomo Rappaccini: Laboratory jacket
Beatrice Rappaccini: Purple shawl, hair clip with purple flower
Lisabetta: Apron, large skeleton key inside apron pocket
Giovanni Guasconti: Text books, large coin in pocket, bouquet of flowers
Professor Pietro Baglioni: Laboratory jacket, small vial inside jacket pocket
Narrators: Dressed in a similar color and style
Tech Crew: Dressed in a similar color and style
Ushers: Dressed in a similar color and style

Staging

The characters are seated in chairs and the narrators on tall stools, all with scripts in hands. This arrangement creates multilevel interest and role separation. See page 3 for a suggested seating diagram that considers character interactions and relationships; however, this is only one of several staging possibilities. Narrators may also be seated in chairs. A small prop table placed between Giovanni and Beatrice holds a bouquet of flowers and a hair clip with attached purple flower.

PowerPoint slides are projected on a screen behind the players to depict each scene (some use the same setting, so there is no need to create seven unique slides). Beginning and ending PowerPoint slides can be designed to display the title of the production as well as the cast and credits. Programs with this and other relevant information can also be created.

Evocative music is played and the lights are dimmed at the beginning and end of the production and during scene breaks. An aroma blend is sprayed during the breaks before Scene 5 and before Scene 7. If desired, spray may also be used lightly before Scene 6.

Suggested Staging Diagram

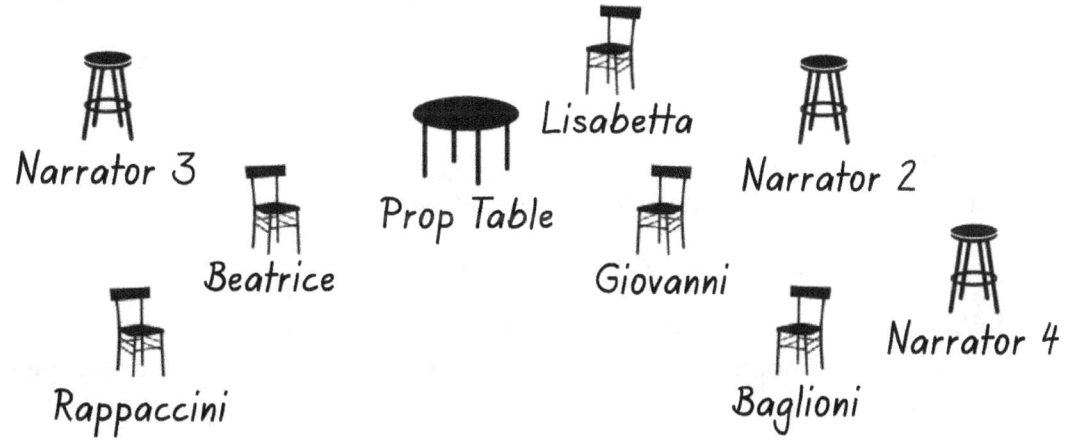

Narrator 1

Narrators are perched on tall stools and characters are seated in chairs. This arrangement adds visual interest and role separation through two height levels.

Audience

Scene 1

NARRATOR ONE *[to audience]:* A long time ago, a young man named Giovanni Guasconti came from Naples, in the south of Italy, to study at the University of Padua. Giovanni did not have much money. He could only afford to rent one room in an old house. In the past, the house had been the palace of a nobleman. This nobleman had met a tragic fate. And that gave Giovanni a strange sense of worry.

LISABETTA: Signor, why do you look sad? Do you find this old mansion gloomy? Put your head out of the window, and you will see sunshine as bright as the sunshine you left behind in Naples.

NARRATOR TWO *[Giovanni looks toward an imaginary window; Narrator Two follows his gaze]:* Giovanni did as Lisabetta, the old housekeeper, said. He saw a garden beneath his window, with plants that seemed to have been cultivated with great care.

GIOVANNI: Does this garden belong to the owner of the house?

LISABETTA: Heaven forbid, signor! No, that garden is cultivated by Signor Giacomo Rappaccini, the famous doctor. It is said that he makes these plants into strong medicines. You might sometimes see the Signor Doctor and maybe even his daughter at work, gathering the strange flowers that grow in the garden.

NARRATOR TWO: In the center of the garden was an old marble fountain. All around it grew plants with gigantic leaves, and some with magnificent flowers. There was one shrub, in particular, that had splendid purple blossoms.

Giovanni heard a rustling of leaves, and saw a tall, sickly looking man working in the garden. He had gray hair, a thin gray beard, and an intelligent but unfriendly face. He did not touch the plants or inhale their aromas. His demeanor was like that of a man walking among savage beasts, or deadly snakes, or evil spirits. He wore thick gloves, and when he came to the purple shrub he placed a mask over his nose and mouth. Then he suddenly stepped back, removed the mask, and called loudly.

RAPPACCINI: Beatrice! Beatrice!

BEATRICE: Here I am, father! Are you in the garden?

NARRATOR THREE *[looks toward Beatrice]:* It was a youthful voice, rich as a tropical sunset and filled with perfume.

RAPPACCINI: Yes, Beatrice, and I need your help.

NARRATOR THREE: A young girl emerged, beautiful as the day. As she came down the garden path, she inhaled the aromas of several of the plants, something her father had avoided.

RAPPACCINI: Beatrice, our splendid treasure needs attention. But it might harm me, so from now on you must be the only one to care for it.

BEATRICE: I will do so gladly.

NARRATOR THREE: She bent towards the shrub and opened her arms as if to embrace it.

BEATRICE *[extends one arm around an imaginary shrub]*: Yes, my sister, it shall be my job to serve you, and you shall reward me with your perfume breath, which to me is the breath of life!

NARRATOR ONE *[to audience]*: As she tenderly cared for the plant, Giovanni watched from above. It seemed to him that, instead of a girl tending her favorite flower, she was one sister caring for another. But soon Doctor Rappaccini signaled to his daughter and together they left the garden.

That night Giovanni dreamed of a splendid flower and a beautiful girl. Flower and girl were different and yet the same. Both were full of some strange danger.

Scene 2

NARRATOR ONE *[to audience]*: When Giovanni awoke, he opened the window and gazed down into the garden that his dreams had made so full of mystery. He was surprised, and a little ashamed, to find how ordinary it appeared.

NARRATOR FOUR *[to Baglioni]*: That day he went to visit Signor Pietro Baglioni, a well-known Professor of Medicine at the university, to whom Giovanni had brought a letter of introduction. The professor was a kind, elderly man. He invited Giovanni to stay for dinner. Giovanni, assuming that men of science who lived in the same city must know each other, mentioned the name of Doctor Rappaccini.

BAGLIONI: He is a greatly skilled doctor. But there are serious problems with his professional character.

GIOVANNI: And what are they?

BAGLIONI: Are you ill? Is that why you are so curious about doctors?

NARRATOR FOUR: Baglioni smiled, as if he knew Giovanni's secret. Then he continued.

BAGLIONI: But, as for Rappaccini, he cares much more for science than for mankind. His patients are interesting to him only as subjects for some new experiment. He would sacrifice human life, even his own, or whatever else was dearest to him, for the sake of adding so much as a tiny seed to the great heap of his knowledge.

GIOVANNI: He must be an awful man, indeed. And yet, esteemed professor, isn't it noble to have such a strong love of science?

BAGLIONI: God forbid! His theory is that all good medicine comes from substances that we call vegetable poisons. These he cultivates with his own hands, and is said to have produced new varieties of poison, more horrible than those occurring in nature.

It is true that now and then he has come up with what seems like a marvelous cure. But, in my opinion, he should receive little credit for such successes—they are probably just good luck—and he should be held responsible for his failures.

GIOVANNI: I don't know how much Doctor Rappaccini loves science, but surely there is something more dear to him. He has a daughter.

BAGLIONI: Aha! So now our friend Giovanni's secret is out!

NARRATOR FOUR: Baglioni laughed and then continued.

BAGLIONI: You have heard of this daughter, whom all the young men in Padua are wild about, though not many have seen her. I know little of the Signora Beatrice, except that Rappaccini is said to have instructed her deeply in his science, and that, young and beautiful as she is, she is already qualified to be a professor. But now, Signor Giovanni, let's drink!

NARRATOR ONE *[to audience]:* Giovanni set out for home thinking of Rappaccini and the beautiful Beatrice. On his way, he passed a florist and bought a fresh bouquet of flowers.

[Lisabetta picks up a bouquet of flowers from the prop table and gives it to Giovanni, who keeps it in his hands until the next scene, when he throws it to Beatrice.]

Scene 3

NARRATOR ONE *[to audience]:* When Giovanni returned home, he sat where he could look down into the garden without being seen. Soon, as Giovanni had half-hoped, half-feared, Beatrice appeared. She seemed even more beautiful than Giovanni had remembered. Her face had an expression of simplicity and sweetness. Giovanni observed a similarity between the splendid shrub with purple blooms and the beautiful girl, for Beatrice had selected colors and arranged her dress to look like the shrub.

NARRATOR THREE *[to Beatrice]:* Approaching the shrub, she threw open her arms and drew its branches into an intimate embrace.

BEATRICE *[extends one arm around an imaginary shrub]:* Give me your breath, my sister, for I am ill from breathing the common air! And give me this flower of yours.

NARRATOR THREE: Beatrice plucked one of the largest blossoms from the shrub and tucked it into her hair. *[Beatrice takes the purple flower from from the prop table and clips it in her hair.]* Just then, a small lizard crept along the path where Beatrice stood. A drop or two of moisture from the broken stem of the flower fell on the lizard's head. The lizard began to shake, then rolled over and died. Beatrice crossed herself sadly, but kept the fatal flower. Giovanni trembled.

GIOVANNI: Am I awake? Have I lost my senses? What is this being? Beautiful? Or terrible?

NARRATOR THREE: A butterfly seemed to be attracted by Beatrice and it fluttered above her head. Beatrice looked up and it fell at her feet, dead. Did the insect die from her breath? Maybe Giovanni had imagined it. Again Beatrice crossed herself sadly.

A sound from Giovanni's room caused Beatrice to look up. She saw Giovanni looking down from his window. Without thinking, Giovanni threw down the bouquet which he had been holding in his hand.

GIOVANNI *[tosses the bouquet of flowers to Beatrice's feet]:* Signora, accept these flowers from Giovanni Guasconti!

BEATRICE *[picks up the bouquet]:* Thank you, signor, I accept your gift. I would like to return the favor with this precious purple flower, but if I toss it into the air, it will not reach you. So, Signor Guasconti, you must be happy with only my thanks.

NARRATOR ONE *[to audience]:* She lifted the bouquet from the ground, and ran quickly out of the garden. It seemed to Giovanni that his beautiful bouquet was beginning to wither in her hand.

[During the scene break Beatrice returns the bouquet to the prop table.]

Scene 4

NARRATOR ONE *[to audience]:* For many days afterward, Giovanni avoided the window that looked into Doctor Rappaccini's garden, as if something horrible would happen if he looked down upon it. Sometimes he tried to forget what he had seen by taking rapid walks through the streets of Padua. But one day someone grabbed him by the arm.

BAGLIONI *[grabs Giovanni's upper arm]*: Signor Giovanni! Stay, my young friend! Have you forgotten me?

NARRATOR FOUR *[to Baglioni]*: It was Baglioni, whom Giovanni had avoided ever since their first meeting. He was afraid the professor would pry too deeply into his secret.

GIOVANNI *[shakes himself free of Baglioni's grasp]*: Yes, I am Giovanni Guasconti. And you are Professor Pietro Baglioni. Now let me pass!

BAGLIONI: Not yet, not yet, Signor Giovanni Guasconti. Stand still. We need to talk.

GIOVANNI: Quickly then, esteemed professor, quickly! Don't you see that I am in a hurry?

NARRATOR TWO *[to Rappaccini]*: While he was speaking, a tall old man walked along the street, moving slowly, as if he was sick. As he passed, he looked intently at Giovanni.

BAGLIONI: It is Doctor Rappaccini! Has he ever seen your face before?

GIOVANNI: Not that I know of.

BAGLIONI: He has seen you! He must have seen you! He is making a study of you. I know that look of his! It is the same look that he has when he bends over a bird, a mouse, or a butterfly, which, while conducting some experiment, he has killed by the perfume of a flower. Signor Giovanni, you are certainly the subject of one of Rappaccini's experiments!

GIOVANNI: Are you trying to make a fool of me? Is *that,* Signor Professor, *your* experiment?

BAGLIONI: Patience, patience! I tell you, my poor Giovanni, that Rappaccini has a scientific interest in you. And the Signora Beatrice? What part does she play in this mystery?

NARRATOR TWO *[to Giovanni]*: But Giovanni, finding Baglioni intolerable, broke away and was gone.

BAGLIONI: This must not be. Rappaccini shall not use him for his hellish experiments!

NARRATOR ONE *[to audience]*: Baglioni looked off in the direction where Giovanni had disappeared, and shook his head. *[Baglioni shakes his head.]*

[Use essential oil spray lightly during the scene break.]

Scene 5

NARRATOR ONE *[to audience]*: When Giovanni reached home he was met by old Lisabetta, who tried to get his attention. She grasped his arm. *[Lisabetta grasps Giovanni's arm.]*

LISABETTA: Signor, signor! Listen, signor! There is a secret entrance into the garden!

GIOVANNI: What did you say? A secret entrance into Doctor Rappaccini's garden?

LISABETTA: Hush! Hush, not so loud! Yes, into the doctor's garden, where you may see all his fine plants. Many young men would give gold to be admitted among those flowers.

GIOVANNI: Show me the way. *[He takes the coin from his pocket and places it in Lisabetta's hand. She, in turn, closes her hand around it and places it in her apron pocket.]*

NARRATOR TWO *[to Lisabetta]*: Lisabetta led him to a door, which she unlocked and opened. *[Lisabetta takes a key out of her apron pocket and mimes unlocking and opening a door. Then she puts the key back into her pocket.]* Giovanni stepped into the garden and stood beneath his own window. He looked around to see if Beatrice or her father were there. Seeing that he was alone, he began to observe the plants. Startled by the rustling of a silk dress, he turned and saw Beatrice. There was surprise in her face, but also pleasure.

BEATRICE: You are a connoisseur of flowers, signor. It is no wonder, therefore, that you were tempted to see my father's rare collection. If he were here, he could tell you many strange and interesting things about these plants, for he has spent a lifetime in such studies, and this garden is his world.

GIOVANNI: And yourself, lady, I have heard you are also deeply skilled in this work.

BEATRICE: Are there really such silly rumors? Do people say that I am skilled in my father's science of plants? What a joke that is! No, though I have grown up among these flowers, I know no more about them than their colors and perfumes, and sometimes I wish I didn't even know that. Signor, do not believe these stories about me. Believe nothing about me except what you see with your own eyes.

NARRATOR THREE *[to Beatrice]*: While Beatrice spoke, there was a delightful fragrance in the air around her. She was happy to spend time with Giovanni. Evidently, her experience of life had been limited to this garden. She talked about things as simple as the daylight or summer clouds, and asked questions about the city, or Giovanni's faraway home, his friends, his mother, and his sisters.

Conversing in this way, they walked toward the splendid shrub with its purple blossoms. Giovanni recognized its fragrance as identical to Beatrice's breath, only more powerful.

NARRATOR THREE: When Beatrice saw the shrub, she spoke to it as if it were human.

BEATRICE: For the first time in my life, I have forgotten you!

GIOVANNI: I remember, signora, you once promised to reward me for the bouquet I gave you, with one of these blossoms. Permit me now to pluck one.

NARRATOR THREE: He made a step towards the shrub, with his hand extended to pluck a flower. But Beatrice rushed forward and caught his hand to stop him, exclaiming in a voice of agony. *[Giovanni mimes reaching for a flower and Beatrice stops him, her thumb on his wrist and her four fingers on the back of his hand; Narrator Three visually follows the action.]*

BEATRICE: Don't touch it! It is fatal!

NARRATOR ONE *[to audience]:* Then she ran away from him and vanished. As Giovanni followed her with his eyes, he saw Doctor Rappaccini, who had been watching them from the shadows. *[Doctor Rappaccini smiles slyly.]*

Scene 6

NARRATOR ONE *[to audience]:* Giovanni awoke the next morning to a burning and tingling pain in his right hand. This was the same hand that Beatrice had held in her own when he was about to pluck one of the purple flowers. On the back of that hand there was a purple print of four small fingers, and on his wrist there was a purple print of a thumb. But Giovanni was so love-struck that he wrapped a handkerchief around his hand and wondered what had stung him. Soon he forgot his pain while thinking about Beatrice.

NARRATOR TWO *[to Giovanni, waving a hand outward from the wrist on the words "second," "third," and "fourth"]:* After the first meeting with Beatrice, there was a second, a third, and a fourth, until meeting Beatrice in the garden was what he lived for. Beatrice felt the same way about Giovanni. And yet they had not kissed, nor held hands, nor even touched but once.

NARRATOR FOUR *[to Baglioni]:* Much time had now passed since Giovanni's last meeting with Baglioni. One morning, however, Giovanni was disagreeably surprised by a visit from the professor. Baglioni chatted for a few moments about the gossip of the city and the university and then brought up another topic.

BAGLIONI: Lately I have been reading the books of a well-known author and found a story of his that interested me. It is about an Indian prince who sent a beautiful woman as a present to Alexander the Great. She was as lovely as the dawn and beautiful as the sunset, but what especially distinguished her was a rich perfume in her breath. Alexander fell in love with her at first sight. Then a doctor discovered her terrible secret.

GIOVANNI: And what was that?

BAGLIONI: That this lovely woman had been nourished with poisons from birth, until her whole body was so full of them that she herself became poisonous. With the rich perfume of her breath, she poisoned the very air. Her love would have been poison, her embrace death! Isn't this a marvelous tale?

GIOVANNI: A childish fable. I am surprised you find time to read such nonsense.

BAGLIONI: By the way, what fragrance is this in your apartment? It is faint, but delicious, and yet I do not like it. If I were to breathe it for long, I think it would make me ill. It is like the breath of a flower. Yet I see no flowers in the chamber.

GIOVANNI: Nor are there any. Nor, I think, is there any fragrance, except in your imagination.

BAGLIONI: My imagination does not often play such tricks. But Rappaccini, I have heard, uses such aromas in his medicines. Likewise, the Signora Beatrice would use the same liquids. Woe to him that drinks them!

NARRATOR TWO: Giovanni's face showed many conflicting emotions, which he tried to control.

GIOVANNI: Signor Professor, perhaps you want to protect me. But, signor, you do not know the Signora Beatrice. So you cannot understand how wrong you are about her character.

BAGLIONI: Giovanni, my poor Giovanni! I know this horrible girl far better than you know her. Now you shall hear the truth about the poisoner Rappaccini and his poisonous daughter. Yes, she is as poisonous as she is beautiful! That old fable of the Indian woman is now true.

NARRATOR TWO: Giovanni groaned and hid his face in his hands.

BAGLIONI: Her father sacrificed his own child in his insane love of science. What will your fate be now, Giovanni? Beyond a doubt, you are selected as the material of some new experiment. Perhaps the result is to be death, perhaps a fate more awful still!

GIOVANNI: It is a dream, surely it is a dream!

BAGLIONI: But do not fear. It is not too late to save yourself. Possibly, we may even succeed in bringing back this miserable child to a normal life. Look at this vial. *[He takes a vial out of his lab coat pocket and holds it up for Giovanni to see.]* One little sip of this antidote will make the most deadly poison useless. Let your Beatrice drink this, and maybe we can stop Rappaccini yet! *[He places the vial on the prop table.]*

NARRATOR ONE *[to audience]:* And with that, Baglioni left the room.

[Use essential oil spray in a stronger intensity during the scene break.]

Scene 7

NARRATOR ONE *[to audience]:* Giovanni decided to create a test that would determine, once and for all, if what Baglioni had said about Beatrice was true. If he could see up close one healthy flower dying in Beatrice's hand, there would be no room for further questions. With this idea, he hurried to the florist's shop and purchased a freshly cut bouquet of flowers. *[Lisabetta takes the bouquet of flowers from the prop table and gives it to Giovanni.]*

NARRATOR TWO *[to Giovanni]:* When it was time for his daily visit with Beatrice, he told himself that her poison had not yet entered his body. Then he noticed that the flowers he held in his hand were already beginning to droop. Horror shot through him. *[Giovanni looks at the bouquet with alarm, then drops it on the floor, where it remains through the end of the production.]* He remembered Baglioni's remark about the fragrance in his room. It must have been the poison in his breath! He saw a spider weaving a web across his window, leaned towards the insect, and breathed upon it. The spider died.

GIOVANNI: Cursed! I am cursed!

NARRATOR THREE *[to Beatrice]:* At that moment a rich, sweet voice came floating up from the garden.

BEATRICE: Giovanni! Giovanni! It is past the hour! Why are you so slow? Come down!

NARRATOR TWO: Giovanni rushed down to Beatrice. A moment ago, he had been full of anger and despair. Yet now, seeing her brought tender emotions.

NARRATOR THREE: Beatrice sensed that something was wrong. They walked on together, sad and silent, until they came to the shrub with the splendid, purple blossoms. Giovanni was frightened by the enjoyment he had in the fragrance of the flowers.

GIOVANNI: Beatrice, where did this plant come from?

BEATRICE: My father created it

GIOVANNI: Created it! Created it! What do you mean, Beatrice?

BEATRICE: At the hour of my birth, this plant sprang from the soil, the result of his scientific work. Do not approach it! It could harm you. But I, dearest Giovanni, I grew up and blossomed with the plant and was nourished by its breath. It was my sister. I loved it with a human affection. Have you suspected it? For me it was an awful doom, the effect of my father's fatal love of science has isolated me from the rest of the world. Until Heaven sent you, dearest Giovanni, how lonely was your poor Beatrice!

NARRATOR TWO: Giovanni now spoke with rage.

GIOVANNI: Cursed one! And finding your loneliness unbearable, you have tempted me into your world of unspeakable horror!

BEATRICE: Giovanni!

GIOVANNI: Yes, poisonous thing! You have done it! You filled my veins with poison! You have made me as deadly as you are. Now we can kiss each other and die!

BEATRICE: Giovanni, why do you say those terrible things to me? It is true that I am the horrible thing you say I am. But you! All you have to do is leave this garden, and forget that there ever was a monster named Beatrice!

GIOVANNI: Do you pretend ignorance? Behold this power that I have gained from the pure daughter of Rappaccini!

NARRATOR TWO: A swarm of insects flitted through the air, and circled round Giovanni's head. He breathed up at them and smiled bitterly at Beatrice as the insects fell down dead.

BEATRICE: I see it! I see it! It is my father's fatal science! No, no, Giovanni, it was not me! Never, never! I only wanted to love you and be with you for a little time, and then to let you leave me, leaving only your memory in my heart. For, Giovanni, although my body is nourished with poison, my spirit craves love as its daily food. It is my father who has united us in this fearful condition. Yes, kill me! Oh, what is death, after what you have said to me?

NARRATOR TWO: Upon hearing her words, Giovanni had a change of heart.

GIOVANNI: Dearest Beatrice, all is not lost. Look! *[He takes the vial from the prop table and holds it up.]* Here is a medicine that a wise doctor gave to me. It is made from plants that are the opposite of your father's poison. Let us drink it together and we will be cured.

BEATRICE: Give it to me! *[She snatches the vial from Giovanni.]* I will drink it first. You must wait to see what happens to me before you drink it.

NARRATOR THREE: She began to drink from the vial. *[Beatrice mimes drinking from the vial. Then she places it on the prop table.]* At the same moment, Rappaccini emerged from the house with a triumphant expression and came slowly towards them. He spread his hand out over them, as if giving a blessing.

RAPPACCINI *[spreading the fingers of his hand above his head and outward in the direction of Beatrice and Giovanni]:* My daughter, you are no longer lonely in the world! Pluck one of these precious blooms from your sister shrub and give it to your bridegroom. It will not harm him now! He now stands apart from ordinary men, as you stand apart from ordinary women. You can now live in the world beloved to one another, and dreadful to all others!

NARRATOR THREE: Beatrice became weaker and weaker. She spoke with her hand upon her heart.

BEATRICE [*places her hand upon her heart*]: Father, why did you doom my life to this misery?

RAPPACCINI: Misery! What do you mean, you foolish girl? Do you think you are doomed to have such marvelous gifts, against which no enemy could triumph? Do you think it is misery to be able to defeat the mightiest person with a single breath? Do you think it is misery to be as terrible as you are beautiful? Would you rather be a weak woman, exposed to all evil and capable of none?

BEATRICE: I would rather have been loved, not feared. But now it does not matter. I am going, father, where the evil which you have tried to make part of me will pass away like a dream. The fragrance of these poisonous flowers will no longer poison my breath. Farewell, Giovanni! Your words of hatred are as heavy as lead within my heart, but they, too, will pass. Oh, was there not, from the start, more poison in your nature than in mine?

NARRATOR THREE: Beatrice sank to the ground. [*Beatrice slumps forward in her chair, head in her lap, and remains in this position through the end of the production.*] As poison had been her life, so the powerful antidote was death. She died there, at the feet of her father and Giovanni.

NARRATOR ONE [*to audience*]: Just at that moment, Baglioni looked out from the window and called out loudly, in a tone of triumph mixed with horror.

BAGLIONI: Rappaccini! Rappaccini! And is *this* the result of your experiment?

THE END

Readers Theater Script with Greek Chorus, Secondary Level

Readers Theater Adaptation of
Hawthorne's "Rappaccini's Daughter"
By Sharon Adelman Reyes

Characters
Doctor Giacomo Rappaccini, a scientist specializing in botany
Beatrice Rappaccini, his daughter
Lisabetta, a housekeeper
Giovanni Guasconti, a student
Professor Pietro Baglioni, of the University of Padua
Narrator One (opens and closes each scene)
Narrator Two (relays action relating to Giovanni)
Narrator Three (relays action relating to Beatrice)
Narrator Four (relays action relating to Baglioni)
Greek Chorus (three or more voices needed)

Pronunciation Key
Doctor Giacomo Rappaccini: JAHK uh mo rahp uh CHEE nee
Giovanni Guasconti: joh VAH nee gwa SKOHN tee
Beatrice Rappaccini: bay ah TREE chay rahp uh CHEE nee
Professor Pietro Baglioni: PYET ro bal YOH nee
Lisabetta: leez uh BET uh
Padua: PAH dwah
Signor: see NYOR
Signora: see NYOR uh

Tech Crew
Lights: Dim at beginning and end of production and between scenes
Music: Play at beginning and end of production and between scenes
Projection: Use PowerPoint slides as backdrops for each scene
Aroma: Spray essential oil formula into the air before Scenes 5 & 7
Ushers: As needed

Props and Costume Pieces

Doctor Giacomo Rappaccini: Laboratory jacket
Beatrice Rappaccini: Purple shawl, hair clip with purple flower
Lisabetta: Apron, large skeleton key inside apron pocket
Giovanni Guasconti: Textbooks, large coin in pocket, bouquet of flowers
Professor Pietro Baglioni: Laboratory jacket, small vial inside jacket pocket
Narrators: Dressed in a similar color and style
Tech Crew: Dressed in a similar color and style
Ushers: Dressed in a similar color and style

Staging

The characters are seated in chairs and the narrators on tall stools, all with scripts in hands. And the Greek Chorus is standing in a semicircle behind the action, creating multilevel interest and role separation. (Traditionally the chorus would have been in an opera pit, but that is not possible in a classroom.) See the diagram on page 3 for a suggested seating arrangement that considers character interactions and relationships; however, this is only one of several staging possibilities. Narrators may also be seated in chairs. A small prop table placed between Giovanni and Beatrice holds a bouquet of flowers and a hair clip with attached purple flower.

PowerPoint slides are projected on a screen behind the players to depict each scene (some use the same setting, so there is no need to create seven unique slides). Beginning and ending PowerPoint slides can be designed to display the title of the production as well as the cast and credits. Programs with this and other relevant information can also be created.

Evocative music is played and the lights are dimmed at the beginning and end of the production and during scene breaks. An aroma blend is sprayed during the breaks before Scene 5 and before Scene 7. If desired, spray may also be used lightly before Scene 6.

Suggested Staging Diagram

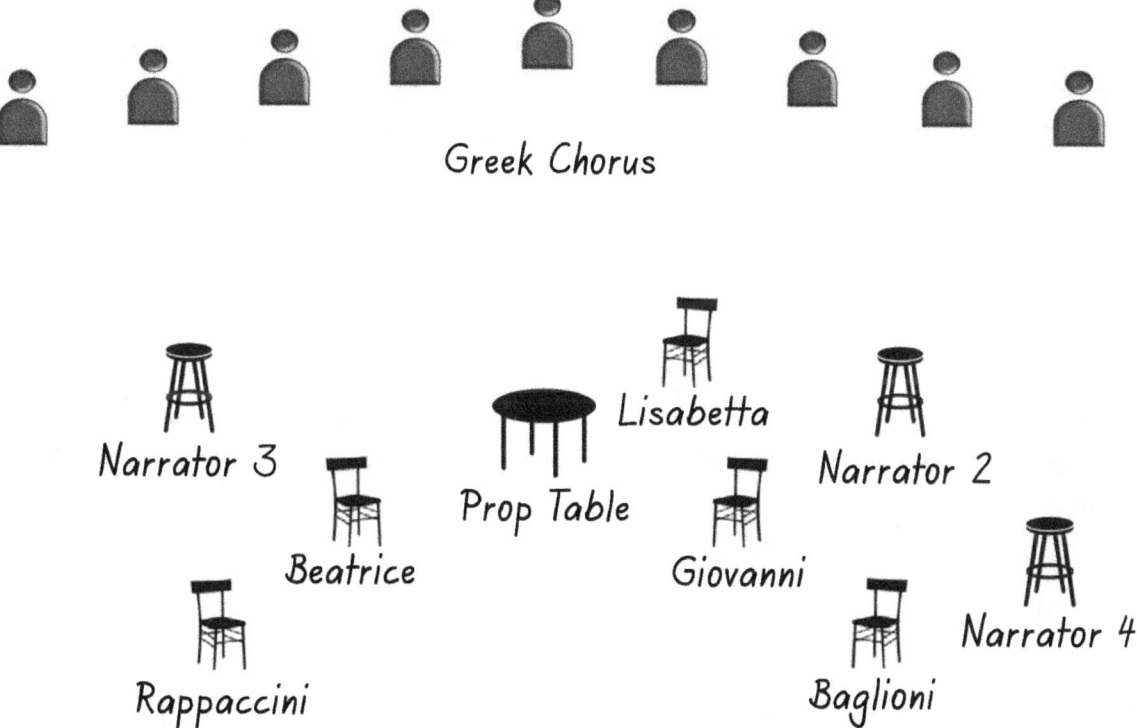

Narrator 1

Narrators are perched on tall stools, characters are seated in chairs, and the Greek chorus stands in a semicircle. This arrangement adds visual interest and role separation through three height levels.

Audience

Scene 1

[The members of the Greek Chorus sit on the floor, motionless and in identical positions, in a large semicircle behind all of the other readers.]

NARRATOR ONE *[to audience]:* A long time ago, a young man named Giovanni Guasconti came from Naples, in the south of Italy, to study at the University of Padua. Giovanni did not have much money. He could only afford to rent one room in an old house. In the past, the house had been the palace of a nobleman. This nobleman had met a tragic fate.

GREEK CHORUS *[speaks while rising in synchronized motion, remains standing until the conclusion of the performance]:* Tragic fate, tragic fate, tragic fate.

NARRATOR ONE *[to audience]:* And that gave Giovanni a strange sense of worry.

GREEK CHORUS *[elongating the vowel sound]:* Fate, fate, fate, fate.

LISABETTA: Signor, why do you look sad? Do you find this old mansion gloomy? Put your head out of the window, and you will see sunshine as bright as the sunshine you left behind in Naples.

NARRATOR TWO *[Giovanni looks toward an imaginary window; Narrator Two follows his gaze]:* Giovanni did as Lisabetta, the old housekeeper, said. He saw a garden beneath his window, with plants that seemed to have been cultivated with great care.

GIOVANNI: Does this garden belong to the owner of the house?

LISABETTA: Heaven forbid, signor! No, that garden is cultivated by Signor Giacomo Rappaccini, the famous doctor. It is said that he makes these plants into strong medicines. You might sometimes see the Signor Doctor and maybe even his daughter at work, gathering the strange flowers that grow in the garden.

NARRATOR TWO: In the center of the garden was an old marble fountain. All around it grew plants with gigantic leaves, and some with magnificent flowers. There was one shrub, in particular, that had splendid purple blossoms.

Giovanni heard a rustling of leaves, and saw a tall, sickly looking man working in the garden. He had gray hair, a thin gray beard, and an intelligent but unfriendly face. He did not touch the plants or inhale their aromas. His demeanor was like that of a man walking among savage beasts, or deadly snakes, or evil spirits. He wore thick gloves, and when he came to the purple shrub he placed a mask over his nose and mouth. Then he suddenly stepped back, removed the mask, and called loudly.

RAPPACCINI: Beatrice! Beatrice!

BEATRICE: Here I am, father! Are you in the garden?

NARRATOR THREE *[looks toward Beatrice]:* It was a youthful voice, rich as a tropical sunset and filled with perfume.

RAPPACCINI: Yes, Beatrice, and I need your help.

NARRATOR THREE: A young girl emerged, beautiful as the day. As she came down the garden path, she inhaled the aromas of several of the plants, something her father had avoided.

GREEK CHORUS: Perfume *[inhaling in unison and then elongating the vowel]*, aaaaahh, perfume.

RAPPACCINI: Beatrice, our splendid treasure needs attention. But it might harm me, so from now on you must be the only one to care for it.

BEATRICE: I will do so gladly.

NARRATOR THREE: She bent towards the shrub and opened her arms as if to embrace it.

BEATRICE *[extends one arm around an imaginary shrub]:* Yes, my sister, it shall be my job to serve you, and you shall reward me with your perfume breath, which to me is the breath of life!

NARRATOR ONE *[to audience]:* As she tenderly cared for the plant, Giovanni watched from above. It seemed to him that, instead of a girl tending her favorite flower, she was one sister caring for another. But soon Doctor Rappaccini signaled to his daughter and together they left the garden.

That night Giovanni dreamed of a splendid flower and a beautiful girl. Flower and girl were different and yet the same. Both were full of some strange danger.

Scene 2

NARRATOR ONE *[to audience]:* When Giovanni awoke, he opened the window and gazed down into the garden that his dreams had made so full of mystery. He was surprised, and a little ashamed, to find how ordinary it appeared.

NARRATOR FOUR *[to Baglioni]:* That day he went to visit Signor Pietro Baglioni, a well-known Professor of Medicine at the university, to whom Giovanni had brought a letter of introduction. The professor was a kind, elderly man. He invited Giovanni to stay for dinner. Giovanni, assuming that men of science who lived in the same city must know each other, mentioned the name of Doctor Rappaccini.

BAGLIONI: He is a greatly skilled doctor. But there are serious problems with his professional character.

GIOVANNI: And what are they?

BAGLIONI: Are you ill? Is that why you are so curious about doctors?

NARRATOR FOUR: Baglioni smiled, as if he knew Giovanni's secret. Then he continued.

BAGLIONI: But, as for Rappaccini, he cares much more for science than for mankind. His patients are interesting to him only as subjects for some new experiment. He would sacrifice human life, even his own, or whatever else was dearest to him, for the sake of adding so much as a tiny seed to the great heap of his knowledge.

GIOVANNI: He must be an awful man, indeed. And yet, esteemed professor, isn't it noble to have such a strong love of science?

BAGLIONI: God forbid! His theory is that all good medicine comes from substances that we call vegetable poisons. These he cultivates with his own hands, and is said to have produced new varieties of poison, more horrible than those occurring in nature.

GREEK CHORUS [softly]: How much should one love science? How much should one love science?

BAGLIONI: It is true that now and then he has come up with what seems like a marvelous cure. But, in my opinion, he should receive little credit for such successes—they are probably just good luck—and he should be held responsible for his failures.

GREEK CHORUS [louder]: How much should one love science? How much should one love science?

GIOVANNI: I don't know how much Doctor Rappaccini loves science, but surely there is something more dear to him. He has a daughter.

BAGLIONI: Aha! So now our friend Giovanni's secret is out!

NARRATOR FOUR: Baglioni laughed and then continued.

BAGLIONI: You have heard of this daughter, whom all the young men in Padua are wild about, though not many have seen her. I know little of the Signora Beatrice, except that Rappaccini is said to have instructed her deeply in his science, and that, young and beautiful as she is, she is already qualified to be a professor. But now, Signor Giovanni, let's drink!

NARRATOR ONE [to audience]: Giovanni set out for home thinking of Rappaccini and the beautiful Beatrice. On his way, he passed a florist and bought a fresh bouquet of flowers.

[Lisabetta picks up a bouquet of flowers from the prop table and gives it to Giovanni, who keeps it in his hands until the next scene, when he throws it to Beatrice.]

Scene 3

NARRATOR ONE *[to audience]:* When Giovanni returned home, he sat where he could look down into the garden without being seen. Soon, as Giovanni had half-hoped, half-feared, Beatrice appeared. She seemed even more beautiful than Giovanni had remembered. Her face had an expression of simplicity and sweetness. Giovanni observed a similarity between the splendid shrub with purple blooms and the beautiful girl, for Beatrice had selected colors and arranged her dress to look like the shrub.

NARRATOR THREE *[to Beatrice]:* Approaching the shrub, she threw open her arms and drew its branches into an intimate embrace.

BEATRICE *[extends one arm around an imaginary shrub]:* Give me your breath, my sister, for I am ill from breathing the common air! And give me this flower of yours.

NARRATOR THREE: Beatrice plucked one of the largest blossoms from the shrub and tucked it into her hair. *[Beatrice takes the purple flower from from the prop table and clips it in her hair.]* Just then, a small lizard crept along the path where Beatrice stood. A drop or two of moisture from the broken stem of the flower fell on the lizard's head. The lizard began to shake, then rolled over and died. Beatrice crossed herself sadly, but kept the fatal flower. Giovanni trembled.

GIOVANNI: Am I awake? Have I lost my senses? What is this being? Beautiful? Or terrible?

GREEK CHORUS *[members raise arms upward in unison, palms toward the ceiling, and remain in this questioning pose]:* Beautiful or terrible? Terrible or beautiful?

NARRATOR THREE: A butterfly seemed to be attracted by Beatrice and it fluttered above her head. Beatrice looked up and it fell at her feet, dead. Did the insect die from her breath? Maybe Giovanni had imagined it. Again Beatrice crossed herself sadly.

GREEK CHORUS *[members lower arms in unison]:* Terrible or beautiful? Beautiful or terrible?

NARRATOR THREE: A sound from Giovanni's room caused Beatrice to look up. She saw Giovanni looking down from his window. Without thinking, Giovanni threw down the bouquet which he had been holding in his hand.

GIOVANNI *[tosses the bouquet of flowers to Beatrice's feet]:* Signora, accept these flowers from Giovanni Guasconti!

BEATRICE *[picks up the bouquet]:* Thank you, signor, I accept your gift. I would like to return the favor with this precious purple flower, but if I toss it into the air, it will not reach you. So, Signor Guasconti, you must be happy with only my thanks.

NARRATOR ONE *[to audience]:* She lifted the bouquet from the ground, and ran quickly out of the garden. It seemed to Giovanni that his beautiful bouquet was beginning to wither in her hand.

[During the scene break Beatrice returns the bouquet to the prop table.]

Scene 4

NARRATOR ONE *[to audience]:* For many days afterward, Giovanni avoided the window that looked into Doctor Rappaccini's garden, as if something horrible would happen if he looked down upon it. Sometimes he tried to forget what he had seen by taking rapid walks through the streets of Padua. But one day someone grabbed him by the arm.

BAGLIONI *[grabs Giovanni's upper arm]:* Signor Giovanni! Stay, my young friend! Have you forgotten me?

NARRATOR FOUR *[to Baglioni]:* It was Baglioni, whom Giovanni had avoided ever since their first meeting. He was afraid the professor would pry too deeply into his secret.

GIOVANNI *[shakes himself free of Baglioni's grasp]:* Yes, I am Giovanni Guasconti. And you are Professor Pietro Baglioni. Now let me pass!

BAGLIONI: Not yet, not yet, Signor Giovanni Guasconti. Stand still. We need to talk.

GIOVANNI: Quickly then, esteemed professor, quickly! Don't you see that I am in a hurry?

NARRATOR TWO *[to Rappaccini]:* While he was speaking, a tall old man walked along the street, moving slowly, as if he was sick. As he passed, he looked intently at Giovanni.

GREEK CHORUS: Giovanni, beware!

BAGLIONI: It is Doctor Rappaccini! Has he ever seen your face before?

GIOVANNI: Not that I know of.

GREEK CHORUS *[all turn in direction of Rappaccini, extending arms and pointing at him]:* Beware, beware!

BAGLIONI: He has seen you! He must have seen you! He is making a study of you. I know that look of his! It is the same look that he has when he bends over a bird, a mouse, or a butterfly, which, while conducting some experiment, he has killed by the perfume of a flower. Signor Giovanni, you are certainly the subject of one of Rappaccini's experiments!

GIOVANNI: Are you trying to make a fool of me? Is *that*, Signor Professor, *your* experiment?

BAGLIONI: Patience, patience! I tell you, my poor Giovanni, that Rappaccini has a scientific interest in you. And the Signora Beatrice? What part does she play in this mystery?

NARRATOR TWO [*to Giovanni*]: But Giovanni, finding Baglioni intolerable, broke away and was gone.

BAGLIONI: This must not be. Rappaccini shall not use him for his hellish experiments!

NARRATOR ONE [*to audience*]: Baglioni looked off in the direction where Giovanni had disappeared, and shook his head. [*Baglioni shakes his head.*]

[*Use essential oil spray lightly during the scene break.*]

Scene 5

NARRATOR ONE [*to audience*]: When Giovanni reached home he was met by old Lisabetta, who tried to get his attention. She grasped his arm.

LISABETTA [*grasps Giovanni's arm*]: Signor, signor! Listen, signor! There is a secret entrance into the garden!

GIOVANNI: What did you say? A secret entrance into Doctor Rappaccini's garden?

LISABETTA: Hush! Hush, not so loud! Yes, into the doctor's garden, where you may see all his fine plants. Many young men would give gold to be admitted among those flowers.

GIOVANNI: Show me the way. [*He takes the coin from his pocket and places it in Lisabetta's hand. She, in turn, closes her hand around it and places it in her apron pocket.*]

NARRATOR TWO [*to Lisabetta*]: Lisabetta led him to a door, which she unlocked and opened. [*Lisabetta takes a key out of her apron pocket and mimes unlocking and opening a door. Then she puts the key back into her pocket.*] Giovanni stepped into the garden and stood beneath his own window. He looked around to see if Beatrice or her father were there. Seeing that he was alone, he began to observe the plants. Startled by the rustling of a silk dress, he turned and saw Beatrice. There was surprise in her face, but also pleasure.

BEATRICE: You are a connoisseur of flowers, signor. It is no wonder, therefore, that you were tempted to see my father's rare collection. If he were here, he could tell you many strange and interesting things about these plants, for he has spent a lifetime in such studies, and this garden is his world.

GIOVANNI: And yourself, lady, I have heard you are also deeply skilled in this work.

BEATRICE: Are there really such silly rumors? Do people say that I am skilled in my father's science of plants? What a joke that is! No, though I have grown up among these flowers, I know no more about them than their colors and perfumes, and sometimes I wish I didn't even know that. Signor, do not believe these stories about me. Believe nothing about me except what you see with your own eyes.

NARRATOR THREE [to Beatrice]: While Beatrice spoke, there was a delightful fragrance in the air around her. She was happy to spend time with Giovanni. Evidently, her experience of life had been limited to this garden. She talked about things as simple as the daylight or summer clouds, and asked questions about the city, or Giovanni's faraway home, his friends, his mother, and his sisters.

Conversing in this way, they walked toward the splendid shrub with its purple blossoms. Giovanni recognized its fragrance as identical to Beatrice's breath, only more powerful.

GREEK CHORUS [sways in unison to the right on the word "beautiful" and to the left on the word "terrible"]: Beautiful or terrible? Terrible or beautiful?

NARRATOR THREE: When Beatrice saw the shrub, she spoke to it as if it were human.

BEATRICE: For the first time in my life, I have forgotten you!

GIOVANNI: I remember, signora, you once promised to reward me for the bouquet I gave you, with one of these blossoms. Permit me now to pluck one.

NARRATOR THREE: He made a step towards the shrub, with his hand extended to pluck a flower. But Beatrice rushed forward and caught his hand to stop him, exclaiming in a voice of agony. [Giovanni mimes reaching for a flower and Beatrice stops him, her thumb on his wrist and her four fingers on the back of his hand; Narrator Three visually follows the action.]

BEATRICE: Don't touch it! It is fatal!

GREEK CHORUS [sway in unison to the right on the word "beautiful" and to the left on the word "terrible"]: Beautiful or terrible? Terrible or beautiful?

NARRATOR ONE [to audience]: Then she ran away from him and vanished. As Giovanni followed her with his eyes, he saw Doctor Rappaccini, who had been watching them from the shadows. [Doctor Rappaccini smiles slyly.]

Scene 6

NARRATOR ONE [to audience]: Giovanni awoke the next morning to a burning and tingling pain in his right hand. This was the same hand that Beatrice had held in her own when he was about to pluck one of the purple flowers. On the back of that hand there was a purple print of four small fingers, and on his wrist there was a purple print of a thumb. But Giovanni was so love-struck that he wrapped a handkerchief around his hand and wondered what had stung him. Soon he forgot his pain while thinking about Beatrice.

GREEK CHORUS: Love *[elongating the vowel]*, aaaaahh, love!

NARRATOR TWO *[to Giovanni, waving a hand outward from the wrist on the words "second," "third," and "fourth"]*: After the first meeting with Beatrice, there was a second, a third, and a fourth, until meeting Beatrice in the garden was what he lived for. Beatrice felt the same way about Giovanni. And yet they had not kissed, nor held hands, nor even touched but once.

GREEK CHORUS: Love *[elongating the vowel]*, aaaaahh, love!

NARRATOR FOUR *[to Baglioni]*: Much time had now passed since Giovanni's last meeting with Baglioni. One morning, however, Giovanni was disagreeably surprised by a visit from the professor. Baglioni chatted for a few moments about the gossip of the city and the university and then brought up another topic.

BAGLIONI: Lately I have been reading the books of a well-known author and found a story of his that interested me. It is about an Indian prince who sent a beautiful woman as a present to Alexander the Great. She was as lovely as the dawn and beautiful as the sunset, but what especially distinguished her was a rich perfume in her breath. Alexander fell in love with her at first sight. Then a doctor discovered her terrible secret.

GIOVANNI: And what was that?

BAGLIONI: That this lovely woman had been nourished with poisons from birth, until her whole body was so full of them that she herself became poisonous. With the rich perfume of her breath, she poisoned the very air. Her love would have been poison, her embrace death! Isn't this a marvelous tale?

GIOVANNI: A childish fable. I am surprised you find time to read such nonsense.

GREEK CHORUS *[all move forearms and hands upward, gesturing a question]*: Is it a fable? Or is it science? Is it imaged? Or is it real?

BAGLIONI: By the way, what fragrance is this in your apartment? It is faint, but delicious, and yet I do not like it. If I were to breathe it for long, I think it would make me ill. It is like the breath of a flower. Yet I see no flowers in the chamber.

GIOVANNI: Nor are there any. Nor, I think, is there any fragrance, except in your imagination.

GREEK CHORUS: Perfume *[inhaling and then elongating the vowel]*, aaaaahh, perfume.

BAGLIONI: My imagination does not often play such tricks. But Rappaccini, I have heard, uses such aromas in his medicines. Likewise, the Signora Beatrice would use the same liquids. Woe to him that drinks them!

NARRATOR TWO: Giovanni's face showed many conflicting emotions, which he tried to control.

GIOVANNI: Signor Professor, perhaps you want to protect me. But, signor, you do not know the Signora Beatrice. So you cannot understand how wrong you are about her character.

BAGLIONI: Giovanni, my poor Giovanni! I know this horrible girl far better than you know her. Now you shall hear the truth about the poisoner Rappaccini and his poisonous daughter. Yes, she is as poisonous as she is beautiful! That old fable of the Indian woman is now true.

NARRATOR TWO: Giovanni groaned and hid his face in his hands.

BAGLIONI: Her father sacrificed his own child in his insane love of science. What will your fate be now, Giovanni? Beyond a doubt, you are selected as the material of some new experiment. Perhaps the result is to be death, perhaps a fate more awful still!

GREEK CHORUS: Tragic fate, tragic fate!

GIOVANNI: It is a dream, surely it is a dream!

GREEK CHORUS: Fate, fate, fate!

BAGLIONI: But do not fear. It is not too late to save yourself. Possibly, we may even succeed in bringing back this miserable child to a normal life. Look at this vial. *[He takes a vial out of his lab coat pocket and holds it up for Giovanni to see.]* One little sip of this antidote will make the most deadly poison useless. Let your Beatrice drink this, and maybe we can stop Rappaccini yet! *[He places the vial on the prop table.]*

NARRATOR ONE *[to audience]*: And with that, Baglioni left the room.

[Use essential oil spray in a stronger intensity during the scene break.]

Scene 7

NARRATOR ONE *[to audience]*: Giovanni decided to create a test that would determine, once and for all, if what Baglioni had said about Beatrice was true. If he could see up close one healthy flower dying in Beatrice's hand, there would be no room for further questions. With this idea, he hurried to the florist's shop and purchased a freshly cut bouquet of flowers. *[Lisabetta takes the bouquet of flowers from the prop table and gives it to Giovanni.]*

GREEK CHORUS: Perfume *[inhaling and then elongating the vowel]*, aaaaahh, perfume.

NARRATOR TWO *[to Giovanni]:* When it was time for his daily visit with Beatrice, he told himself that her poison had not yet entered his body. Then he noticed that the flowers he held in his hand were already beginning to droop. Horror shot through him. *[Giovanni looks at the bouquet with alarm, then drops it on the floor, where it remains through the end of the production.]* He remembered Baglioni's remark about the fragrance in his room. It must have been the poison in his breath! He saw a spider weaving a web across his window, leaned towards the insect, and breathed upon it. The spider died.

GIOVANNI: Cursed! I am cursed!

GREEK CHORUS: Poisoned, you are poisoned!

NARRATOR THREE *[to Beatrice]:* At that moment a rich, sweet voice came floating up from the garden.

BEATRICE: Giovanni! Giovanni! It is past the hour! Why are you so slow? Come down!

NARRATOR TWO: Giovanni rushed down to Beatrice. A moment ago, he had been full of anger and despair. Yet now, seeing her brought tender emotions.

GREEK CHORUS: Love *[elongating the vowel]*, aaaaahh, love!

NARRATOR THREE: Beatrice sensed that something was wrong. They walked on together, sad and silent, until they came to the shrub with the splendid, purple blossoms. Giovanni was frightened by the enjoyment he had in the fragrance of the flowers.

GIOVANNI: Beatrice, where did this plant come from?

BEATRICE: My father created it

GIOVANNI: Created it! Created it! What do you mean, Beatrice?

BEATRICE: At the hour of my birth, this plant sprang from the soil, the result of his scientific work.

GREEK CHORUS: Beware, beware!

BEATRICE: Do not approach it! It could harm you. But I, dearest Giovanni, I grew up and blossomed with the plant and was nourished by its breath. It was my sister. I loved it with a human affection. Have you suspected it? For me it was an awful doom, the effect of my father's fatal love of science has isolated me from the rest of the world. Until Heaven sent you, dearest Giovanni, how lonely was your poor Beatrice!

NARRATOR TWO: Giovanni now spoke with rage.

GIOVANNI: Cursed one! And finding your loneliness unbearable, you have tempted me into your world of unspeakable horror!

BEATRICE: Giovanni!

GIOVANNI: Yes, poisonous thing! You have done it! You filled my veins with poison! You have made me as deadly as you are. Now we can kiss each other and die!

BEATRICE: Giovanni, why do you say those terrible things to me? It is true that I am the horrible thing you say I am. But you! All you have to do is leave this garden, and forget that there ever was a monster named Beatrice!

GIOVANNI: Do you pretend ignorance? Behold this power that I have gained from the pure daughter of Rappaccini!

NARRATOR TWO: A swarm of insects flitted through the air, and circled round Giovanni's head. He breathed up at them and smiled bitterly at Beatrice as the insects fell down dead.

GREEK CHORUS: Poison! Poison!

BEATRICE: I see it! I see it! It is my father's fatal science! No, no, Giovanni, it was not me! Never, never! I only wanted to love you and be with you for a little time, and then to let you leave me, leaving only your memory in my heart. For, Giovanni, although my body is nourished with poison, my spirit craves love as its daily food. It is my father who has united us in this fearful condition. Yes, kill me! Oh, what is death, after what you have said to me?

NARRATOR TWO: Upon hearing her words, Giovanni had a change of heart.

GREEK CHORUS: Love *[elongating the vowel]*, aaaaahh, love!

GIOVANNI: Dearest Beatrice, all is not lost. Look! *[He takes the vial from the prop table and holds it up.]* Here is a medicine that a wise doctor gave to me. It is made from plants that are the opposite of your father's poison. Let us drink it together and we will be cured.

GREEK CHORUS: Don't drink it! Don't drink it!

BEATRICE: Give it to me! *[She snatches the vial from Giovanni.]* I will drink it first. You must wait to see what happens to me before you drink it.

GREEK CHORUS *[louder, more insistent]*: Don't drink it! Don't drink it!

NARRATOR THREE: She began to drink from the vial. *[Beatrice mimes drinking from the vial. Then she places it on the prop table.]* At the same moment, Rappaccini emerged from the house with a triumphant expression and came slowly towards them. He spread his hand out over them, as if giving a blessing.

RAPPACCINI *[spreading the fingers of his hand above his head and outward in the direction of Beatrice and Giovanni]*: My daughter, you are no longer lonely in the world! Pluck one of these precious blooms from your sister shrub and give it to your bridegroom. It will not harm him now! He now stands apart from ordinary men, as you stand apart from ordinary women. You can now live in the world beloved to one another, and dreadful to all others!

GREEK CHORUS: Beloved and dreadful, dreadful, dreadful, dreadful!

NARRATOR THREE: Beatrice became weaker and weaker. She spoke with her hand upon her heart.

BEATRICE *[places her hand upon her heart]*: Father, why did you doom my life to this misery?

GREEK CHORUS *[wailing, raising arms and hands upward, swaying from left to right with each recitation of the word "misery"]*: Doom and misery, misery, misery, misery!

RAPPACCINI: Misery! What do you mean, you foolish girl? Do you think you are doomed to have such marvelous gifts, against which no enemy could triumph? Do you think it is misery to be able to defeat the mightiest person with a single breath? Do you think it is misery to be as terrible as you are beautiful? Would you rather be a weak woman, exposed to all evil and capable of none?

BEATRICE: I would rather have been loved, not feared. But now it does not matter. I am going, father, where the evil which you have tried to make part of me will pass away like a dream. The fragrance of these poisonous flowers will no longer poison my breath. Farewell, Giovanni! Your words of hatred are as heavy as lead within my heart, but they, too, will pass. Oh, was there not, from the start, more poison in your nature than in mine?

GREEK CHORUS: Who really is the poisonous one? Who really is the poisonous one?

NARRATOR THREE: Beatrice sank to the ground. *[Beatrice slumps forward in her chair, head in her lap, and remains in this position through the end of the production.]* As poison had been her life, so the powerful antidote was death. She died there, at the feet of her father and Giovanni.

NARRATOR ONE *[to audience]:* Just at that moment, Baglioni looked out from the window and called out loudly, in a tone of triumph mixed with horror.

BAGLIONI: Rappaccini! Rappaccini! And is *this* the result of your experiment?

GREEK CHORUS *[in synchronized motion, all members sink back to the floor, lower heads onto laps, as if to vanish under their robes]*: How much should one love science? How much should one love science? *[Gradually fade out.]* Science, science, science, science, science, science . . .

THE END

Readers Theater Script, Middle School Level

Readers Theater Adaptation of
Hawthorne's "Rappaccini's Daughter"
By Sharon Adelman Reyes

Characters
Doctor Giacomo Rappaccini, a scientist specializing in botany
Beatrice Rappaccini, his daughter
Lisabetta, a housekeeper
Giovanni Guasconti, a student
Professor Pietro Baglioni, of the University of Padua
Narrator One (opens and closes each scene)
Narrator Two (relays action relating to Giovanni)
Narrator Three (relays action relating to Beatrice)
Narrator Four (relays action relating to Baglioni)

Pronunciation Key
Doctor Giacomo Rappaccini: JAHK uh mo rahp uh CHEE nee
Giovanni Guasconti: joh VAH nee gwa SKOHN tee
Beatrice Rappaccini: bay ah TREE chay rahp uh CHEE nee
Professor Pietro Baglioni: PYET ro bal YOH nee
Lisabetta: leez uh BET uh
Padua: PAH dwah
Signor: see NYOR
Signora: see NYOR uh

Tech Crew
Lights: Dim at beginning and end of production and between scenes
Music: Play at beginning and end of production and between scenes
Projection: Use PowerPoint slides as backdrops for each scene
Aroma: Spray essential oil formula into the air before Scenes 5 & 7
Ushers: As needed

Props and Costume Pieces

Doctor Giacomo Rappaccini: Laboratory jacket
Beatrice Rappaccini: Purple shawl, hair clip with purple flower
Lisabetta: Apron, large skeleton key inside apron pocket
Giovanni Guasconti: Textbooks, large coin in pocket, bouquet of flowers
Professor Pietro Baglioni: Laboratory jacket, small vial inside jacket pocket
Narrators: Dressed in a similar color and style
Tech Crew: Dressed in a similar color and style
Ushers: Dressed in a similar color and style

Staging

The characters are seated in chairs and the narrators on tall stools, all with scripts in hands. This arrangement creates multilevel interest and role separation. See page 3 for a suggested seating diagram that considers character interactions and relationships; however, this is only one of several staging possibilities. Narrators may also be seated in chairs. A small prop table placed between Giovanni and Beatrice holds a bouquet of flowers and a hair clip with attached purple flower.

PowerPoint slides are projected on a screen behind the players to depict each scene (some use the same setting, so there is no need to create seven unique slides). Beginning and ending PowerPoint slides can be designed to display the title of the production as well as the cast and credits. Programs with this and other relevant information can also be created.

Evocative music is played and the lights are dimmed at the beginning and end of the production and during scene breaks. An aroma blend is sprayed during the breaks before Scene 5 and before Scene 7. If desired, spray may also be used lightly before Scene 6.

Suggested Staging Diagram

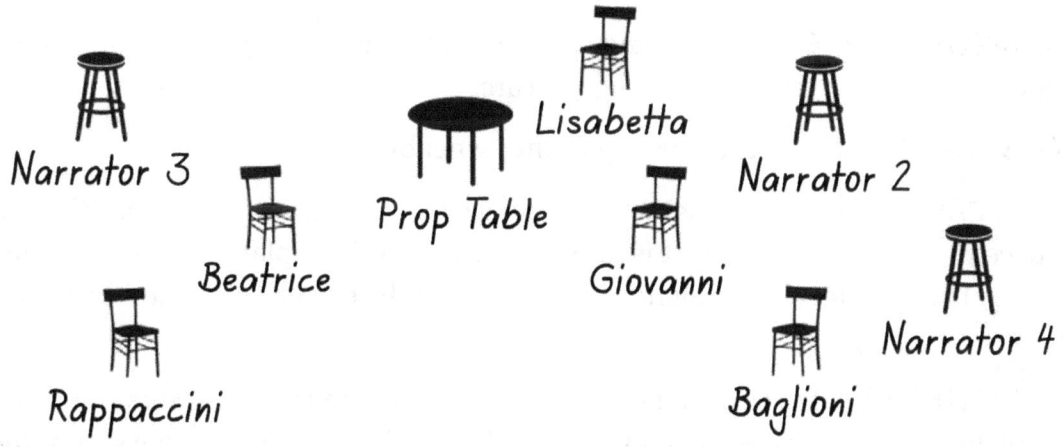

Narrator 1

Narrators are perched on tall stools and characters are seated in chairs. This arrangement adds visual interest and role separation through two height levels.

Audience

Scene 1

NARRATOR ONE: A long time ago, a young man named Giovanni Guasconti came from Naples, in the south of Italy, to study at the University of Padua. Giovanni did not have much money. He could only afford to rent one room in an old house. In the past, the house had been the palace of a nobleman who had met a tragic fate. So Giovanni had a strange sense of worry.

LISABETTA: Signor, why do you look sad? Do you find this old mansion gloomy? Look out the window, and you will see sunshine as bright as the sunshine you left behind in Naples.

NARRATOR TWO: Giovanni looked out the window. He saw a garden with plants that seemed to have been cultivated with great care.

GIOVANNI: Does this garden belong to the owner of the house?

LISABETTA: Heaven forbid, signor! No, that garden is cultivated by Signor Giacomo Rappaccini, the famous doctor. It is said that he makes these plants into strong medicines. You might sometimes see the Signor Doctor and maybe even his daughter at work in the garden.

NARRATOR TWO: In the center of the garden was an old marble fountain. All around it grew plants with gigantic leaves and some with magnificent flowers. One shrub stood out from the others, with its splendid purple blossoms.

Giovanni saw a tall, sickly looking man working in the garden. He had gray hair, a thin gray beard, and an unfriendly face. He did not touch the plants or inhale their aromas. He wore thick gloves. When he came to the purple shrub, he placed a mask over his nose and mouth. He stepped back suddenly, removed the mask, and called loudly.

RAPPACCINI: Beatrice! Beatrice!

BEATRICE: Here I am, father!

NARRATOR THREE: It was a youthful voice, rich as a tropical sunset and filled with perfume.

RAPPACCINI: Beatrice, I need your help.

NARRATOR THREE: A beautiful young girl came down the garden path, inhaling the aromas of the plants.

RAPPACCINI: Beatrice, our splendid treasure needs attention. But it might harm me, so from now on you must be the only one to care for it.

BEATRICE: I will do so gladly.

NARRATOR THREE: She bent towards the purple shrub and opened her arms, as if to embrace it.

BEATRICE: Yes, my sister, I shall serve you, and you shall reward me with your perfume breath, which to me is the breath of life!

NARRATOR ONE: It seemed to Giovanni that, instead of a girl tending her favorite flower, she was one sister caring for another. That night Giovanni dreamed of a splendid flower and a beautiful girl. Flower and girl were different and yet the same. Both were full of some strange danger.

Scene 2

NARRATOR ONE: When Giovanni awoke, he opened the window and gazed down into the garden that his dreams had made so full of mystery. He was surprised that it now looked so ordinary.

NARRATOR FOUR: That day he went to visit Signor Pietro Baglioni, a well-known Professor of Medicine at the university and a friend of Giovanni's father. Giovanni mentioned Doctor Rappaccini.

BAGLIONI: He is a greatly skilled doctor. But there are serious problems with his professional character.

GIOVANNI: And what are they?

BAGLIONI: Are you ill? Is that why you are so curious about doctors?

NARRATOR FOUR: Baglioni smiled, as if he knew Giovanni's secret.

BAGLIONI: Rappaccini cares much more for science than for mankind. His patients are interesting to him only as subjects for some new experiment. He would sacrifice human life, even his own, or whatever else was dearest to him, in order to add to his scientific knowledge.

GIOVANNI: He must be an awful man. And yet, esteemed professor, isn't it noble to have such a strong love of science?

BAGLIONI: God forbid! His theory is that all good medicine comes from vegetable poisons. He is said to have produced new varieties of poison, more horrible than those occurring in nature. Now and then he has come up with what seems like a marvelous cure. But, in my opinion, he should receive little credit for such successes—they are probably just good luck—and he should be held responsible for his failures.

GIOVANNI: Surely there is something more dear to him than science. He has a daughter.

BAGLIONI: Aha! So now our friend Giovanni's secret is out!

NARRATOR FOUR: Baglioni laughed and then continued.

BAGLIONI: You have heard of this daughter, whom all the young men in Padua are wild about, though not many have seen her. I know little of the Signora Beatrice, except that Rappaccini is said to have instructed her deeply in his science, and that, young as she is, she is already qualified to be a professor. But now, Signor Giovanni, let's drink!

NARRATOR ONE: Giovanni returned to his room thinking of Rappaccini and the beautiful Beatrice. On his way home he stopped and bought a fresh bouquet of flowers. *[Lisabetta takes the bouquet of flowers from the prop table and gives it to Giovanni. He keeps the bouquet in his hands until the next scene, when he throws it to Beatrice.]*

Scene 3

NARRATOR ONE: When Giovanni returned home, he sat where he could look down into the garden without being seen. Soon Beatrice appeared, even more beautiful than before. She had selected colors and arranged her dress to look like the shrub.

NARRATOR THREE: Approaching the shrub, Beatrice opened her arms and drew its branches into an intimate embrace.

BEATRICE: Give me your breath, my sister, for I am ill from breathing the common air! And give me this flower of yours.

NARRATOR THREE: Beatrice plucked one of the largest blossoms from the shrub and tucked it into her hair. *[Beatrice takes a purple flower from the prop table and puts it in her hair.]* Just then, a small lizard crept along the path where Beatrice stood. A drop of moisture from the broken flower stem fell on the lizard's head. The lizard began to shake, then rolled over and died. Beatrice crossed herself sadly, but kept the fatal flower. Giovanni trembled.

GIOVANNI: Am I awake? Have I lost my mind? What is this being? Beautiful? Or terrible?

NARRATOR THREE: A butterfly, attracted by Beatrice, fluttered above her head. Beatrice looked up and it fell at her feet, dead. Did it die from her breath? Again Beatrice crossed herself sadly.

A sound from Giovanni's room caused Beatrice to look up. Without thinking, Giovanni threw down the bouquet which he had been holding in his hand. *[Giovanni throws the bouquet of flowers to Beatrice's feet.]*

GIOVANNI: Signora, accept these flowers from Giovanni Guasconti!

BEATRICE *[picks up the bouquet]:* Thank you, signor, I accept your gift. I would like to return the favor with this precious purple flower, but if I toss it into the air, it will not reach you. So, Signor Guasconti, you must be happy with only my thanks.

NARRATOR ONE: She picked up the bouquet and ran quickly out of the garden. It seemed to Giovanni that his beautiful bouquet was beginning to wither in her hand.

[During the scene break she returns the bouquet to the prop table.]

Scene 4

NARRATOR ONE: For many days afterward, Giovanni avoided the window above Doctor Rappaccini's garden. Sometimes he tried to forget what he had seen by taking rapid walks through the streets of Padua. But one day someone grabbed him by the arm.

BAGLIONI *[grabs Giovanni's upper arm]:* Signor Giovanni! Have you forgotten me?

NARRATOR FOUR: It was Baglioni, whom Giovanni had avoided. He was afraid the professor would pry too deeply into his secret.

GIOVANNI *[shakes himself free of Baglioni's grasp]:* Yes, I am Giovanni Guasconti. And you are Professor Pietro Baglioni. Now let me pass!

BAGLIONI: Not yet, not yet, Signor Giovanni Guasconti. Stand still. We need to talk.

GIOVANNI: Quickly, then, esteemed professor, quickly! Don't you see that I am in a hurry?

NARRATOR TWO: While he was speaking, a tall, sickly old man walked slowly by, looking intently at Giovanni.

BAGLIONI: It is Doctor Rappaccini! Has he ever seen you before?

GIOVANNI: Not that I know of.

BAGLIONI: He has seen you! He is making a study of you. I know that look of his! It is the same look that he has when he bends over a bird, a mouse, or a butterfly that he has killed with the perfume of a flower. Signor Giovanni, you are certainly the subject of one of Rappaccini's experiments!

GIOVANNI: Are you trying to make a fool of me? Is *that*, Signor Professor, *your* experiment?

BAGLIONI: Poor Giovanni! Rappaccini has a scientific interest in you. What part does the Signora Beatrice play in this mystery?

NARRATOR TWO: But Giovanni broke away and was gone.

BAGLIONI: This must not be. Rappaccini shall not use him for his hellish experiments!

NARRATOR ONE: Baglioni looked off in the direction where Giovanni had disappeared, and shook his head. *[Baglioni shakes his head.]*

[Use essential oil spray lightly during the scene break.]

Scene 5

NARRATOR ONE: When Giovanni reached home he was met by old Lisabetta, who tried to get his attention.

LISABETTA *[grasps Giovanni's arm]*: Signor, signor! Listen, signor! There is a secret entrance into the garden!

GIOVANNI: A secret entrance into Doctor Rappaccini's garden?

LISABETTA: Hush! Hush, not so loud! Yes, into the doctor's garden, where you may see all his fine plants. Many young men would give gold to be admitted among those flowers.

GIOVANNI: Show me the way. *[He places a coin in Lisabetta's hand. She closes her hand around it and places it in her apron pocket.]*

NARRATOR TWO: Lisabetta led him to a door, which she unlocked and opened. *[Lisabetta takes a key out of her apron pocket and mimes unlocking and opening a door. Then she puts the key back into her pocket.]* Giovanni stepped into the garden. Looking at the plants, he turned and saw Beatrice. There was surprise in her face, but also pleasure.

BEATRICE: You are a connoisseur of flowers, signor. No wonder you were tempted to see my father's rare collection. If he were here, he could tell you many strange and interesting things about these plants.

GIOVANNI: And yourself, lady, I have heard you are also deeply skilled in this work.

BEATRICE: Are there really such silly rumors? I have grown up among these flowers, but I know no more about them than their colors and perfumes, and sometimes I wish I didn't even know that. Signor, do not believe these stories about me. Believe nothing about me except what you see with your own eyes.

NARRATOR THREE: Beatrice was happy to spend time talking to Giovanni. Her experience of life had been limited to this garden, so she asked many questions about the outside world. As she spoke, there was a delightful fragrance in the air around her.

When they came to the shrub with splendid purple blossoms, Giovanni recognized its fragrance as identical to Beatrice's breath, only more powerful. Beatrice spoke to the shrub as if it was human.

BEATRICE: For the first time in my life, I have forgotten you!

GIOVANNI: Signora, you once promised to reward me for the bouquet I gave you, with one of these blossoms. Permit me now to pluck one.

NARRATOR THREE: He made a step towards the shrub, with his hand extended to pluck a flower. But Beatrice rushed forward and caught his hand to stop him, exclaiming in agony. *[Giovanni mimes reaching for a flower and Beatrice stops him with her hand.]*

BEATRICE: Don't touch it! It is fatal!

NARRATOR ONE: Then she ran away from him and vanished. As Giovanni followed her with his eyes, he saw Doctor Rappaccini, who had been watching them from the shadows. *[Doctor Rappaccini smiles slyly.]*

Scene 6

NARRATOR ONE: Giovanni awoke the next morning to a burning and tingling pain in the hand that Beatrice had touched. It now had a purple print of four small fingers, and his wrist had a purple print of a thumb. But Giovanni was so love-struck that he wrapped a handkerchief around his hand and wondered what had stung him. Soon he forgot his pain while thinking about Beatrice.

NARRATOR TWO: After the first meeting with Beatrice, there was a second, a third, and a fourth, until meeting Beatrice in the garden was what he lived for. Beatrice felt the same way about Giovanni. And yet they had not kissed, nor held hands, nor even touched but once.

NARRATOR FOUR: One morning Giovanni had an unexpected visit from Professor Baglioni, who soon brought up a troubling topic.

BAGLIONI: I have been reading an old fable about an Indian prince who sent a beautiful woman, with rich perfumed breath, to Alexander the Great. Alexander fell in love with her at first sight. Then a doctor discovered her terrible secret.

GIOVANNI: And what was that?

BAGLIONI: She had been nourished with poisons from birth until her whole body was so full of them, that she herself had become poisonous. With the rich perfume of her breath, she poisoned the very air. Her love would have been poison, her embrace death! Isn't this a marvelous tale?

GIOVANNI: A childish fable. I am surprised you find time to read such nonsense.

BAGLIONI: What fragrance is this in your apartment? It is faint, but delicious. And yet, I do not like it. If I were to breathe it for long, I think it would make me ill. It is like the breath of a flower. Yet I see no flowers here.

GIOVANNI: Nor are there any. Nor, I think, is there any fragrance, except in your imagination.

BAGLIONI: My imagination does not often play such tricks. But Rappaccini, I have heard, uses such aromas in his medicines. Likewise, the Signora Beatrice would use the same liquids. But beware if you drink them!

GIOVANNI: Signor, you do not know the Signora Beatrice. So you cannot understand how wrong you are about her character.

BAGLIONI: Giovanni, my poor Giovanni! Now you shall hear the truth about the poisoner Rappaccini and his poisonous daughter. Yes, she is as poisonous as she is beautiful! That old fable of the Indian woman is now true.

NARRATOR FOUR: Giovanni groaned and hid his face.

BAGLIONI: Her father sacrificed his own child in his insane love of science. What will your fate be now, Giovanni? Beyond a doubt, you are selected for some new experiment. Perhaps the result is to be death, perhaps a fate more awful still!

GIOVANNI: It is a dream. Surely, it is a dream!

BAGLIONI: Do not fear. It is not too late to save yourself and maybe Beatrice as well. Look at this vial. *[He takes a vial out of his lab coat pocket and holds it up for Giovanni to see.]* One little sip of this antidote will make the most deadly poison useless. Let your Beatrice drink this, and maybe we can stop Rappaccini yet! *[He places the vial on the prop table.]*

NARRATOR ONE: And with that, Baglioni left the room.

[Use essential oil spray in a stronger intensity during the scene break.]

Scene 7

NARRATOR ONE: Giovanni decided to create a test that would decide, once and for all, if Beatrice was really poisonous. If he could see, up close, one healthy flower dying in her hand, he would know the truth. So he purchased a freshly cut bouquet of flowers. *[Lisabetta takes a bouquet of flowers from the prop table and gives it to Giovanni.]*

NARRATOR TWO: But by the time he got home, the flowers were beginning to droop. Could there be poison in his breath? He saw a spider on his window. Giovanni breathed on it and the spider died.

GIOVANNI: Cursed! I am cursed!

NARRATOR THREE: At that moment a rich, sweet voice came floating up from the garden

BEATRICE: Giovanni! Giovanni! Why are you so slow? Come down!

NARRATOR TWO: Giovanni rushed down. He had been full of anger and despair, but seeing Beatrice brought tender emotions. Beatrice sensed that something was wrong. They walked on together, sad and silent, until they came to the shrub with the purple blossoms. Giovanni was frightened by the enjoyment he had in their fragrance.

GIOVANNI: Beatrice, where did this plant come from?

BEATRICE: My father created it

GIOVANNI: Created it! Created it! What do you mean, Beatrice?

BEATRICE: At the hour of my birth, this plant grew from the soil, the result of his scientific work. Do not approach it! It could harm you. But I grew up with the plant and was nourished by its breath. I loved it as my sister. Have you suspected it? For me it was an awful doom. My father's fatal love of science has isolated me from the rest of the world. Until Heaven sent you, dearest Giovanni, I was so lonely!

NARRATOR TWO: Giovanni's now spoke with rage.

GIOVANNI: Cursed one! And finding your loneliness unbearable, you have tempted me into your world of unspeakable horror!

BEATRICE: Giovanni!

GIOVANNI: Yes, poisonous thing! You have done it! You have made me as poisonous as you are. Now we can kiss each other and die!

BEATRICE: Giovanni, why do you say those terrible things to me? It is true that I am the horrible thing you say I am. But all you have to do is leave this garden and forget that there ever was a monster named Beatrice!

GIOVANNI: Do you pretend ignorance? Behold the power you have given me!

NARRATOR TWO: A swarm of insects flitted above Giovanni's head. He breathed up at them and smiled bitterly at Beatrice as the insects fell down dead.

BEATRICE: I see it! It is my father's fatal science! Giovanni, it was not me! I only wanted to love you and be with you for a little time, and then to let you leave me, leaving only your memory in my heart. For, Giovanni, although my body is nourished with poison, my spirit craves love. Yes, kill me! Oh, what is death, after what you have said to me?

NARRATOR TWO: Upon hearing her words, Giovanni had a change of heart.

GIOVANNI: Dearest Beatrice, all is not lost. Look! *[He takes the vial from the prop table and holds it up.]* Here is a potion that will cure of us. Let us drink it together.

BEATRICE: Give it to me! *[She snatches the vial from Giovanni.]* I will drink it first. Wait to see what happens to me before you drink it. *[She mimes drinking from the vial. Then she places it on the prop table.]*

NARRATOR THREE: Rappaccini emerged from the house with a triumphant expression and walked slowly towards them.

RAPPACCINI: My daughter, you are no longer lonely in the world! Pluck one of these precious blooms from your sister shrub and give it to your bridegroom. It will not harm him now! He now stands apart from ordinary men, as you stand apart from ordinary women. You can now live in the world beloved to one another and dreadful to all others!

NARRATOR THREE: Beatrice became weaker and weaker.

BEATRICE *[puts her hand over her heart]*: Father, why did you doom my life to this misery?

RAPPACCINI: Misery! What do you mean, you foolish girl? Do you think you are doomed to have gifts against which no enemy could triumph? Do you think it is misery to be able to defeat the mightiest person with a single breath, to be as terrible as you are beautiful? Would you rather be a weak woman, exposed to all evil and capable of none?

BEATRICE: I would rather have been loved, not feared. But now it does not matter. The fragrance of these flowers will no longer poison my breath. Farewell, Giovanni! Your words of hatred are as heavy as lead within my heart. Oh, was there not more poison in your nature than in mine?

NARRATOR THREE: Beatrice sank to the ground. Her life had been poison and the only possible cure was death. She died there, at the feet of her father and Giovanni.

NARRATOR ONE: Just at that moment, Baglioni looked out from the window and called out loudly, in a tone of triumph mixed with horror.

BAGLIONI: Rappaccini! Rappaccini! And is *this* the result of your experiment?

THE END

Readers Theater Script with Greek Chorus, Basic Level

Readers Theater Adaptation of
Hawthorne's "Rappaccini's Daughter"
By Sharon Adelman Reyes

Characters
Doctor Giacomo Rappaccini, a scientist specializing in botany
Beatrice Rappaccini, his daughter
Lisabetta, a housekeeper
Giovanni Guasconti, a student
Professor Pietro Baglioni, of the University of Padua
Narrator One (opens and closes each scene)
Narrator Two (relays action relating to Giovanni)
Narrator Three (relays action relating to Beatrice)
Narrator Four (relays action relating to Baglioni)
Greek Chorus (three or more voices needed)

Pronunciation Key
Doctor Giacomo Rappaccini: JAHK uh mo rahp uh CHEE nee
Giovanni Guasconti: joh VAH nee gwa SKOHN tee
Beatrice Rappaccini: bay ah TREE chay rahp uh CHEE nee
Professor Pietro Baglioni: PYET ro bal YOH nee
Lisabetta: leez uh BET uh
Padua: PAH dwah
Signor: see NYOR
Signora: see NYOR uh

Tech Crew
Lights: Dim at beginning and end of production and between scenes
Music: Play at beginning and end of production and between scenes
Projection: Use PowerPoint slides as backdrops for each scene
Aroma: Spray essential oil formula into the air before Scenes 5 & 7
Ushers: As needed

Props and Costume Pieces

Doctor Giacomo Rappaccini: Laboratory jacket
Beatrice Rappaccini: Purple shawl, hair clip with purple flower
Lisabetta: Apron, large skeleton key inside apron pocket
Giovanni Guasconti: Textbooks, large coin in pocket, bouquet of flowers
Professor Pietro Baglioni: Laboratory jacket, small vial inside jacket pocket
Narrators: Dressed in a similar color and style
Tech Crew: Dressed in a similar color and style
Ushers: Dressed in a similar color and style

Staging

The characters are seated in chairs and the narrators on tall stools, all with scripts in hands. And the Greek Chorus is standing in a semicircle behind the action, creating multilevel interest and role separation. (Traditionally the chorus would have been in an opera pit, but that is not possible in a classroom.) See the diagram on page 3 for a suggested seating arrangement that considers character interactions and relationships; however, this is only one of several staging possibilities. Narrators may also be seated in chairs. A small prop table placed between Giovanni and Beatrice holds a bouquet of flowers and a hair clip with attached purple flower.

PowerPoint slides are projected on a screen behind the players to depict each scene (some use the same setting, so there is no need to create seven unique slides). Beginning and ending PowerPoint slides can be designed to display the title of the production as well as the cast and credits. Programs with this and other relevant information can also be created.

Evocative music is played and the lights are dimmed at the beginning and end of the production and during scene breaks. An aroma blend is sprayed during the breaks before Scene 5 and before Scene 7. If desired, spray may also be used lightly before Scene 6.

Suggested Staging Diagram

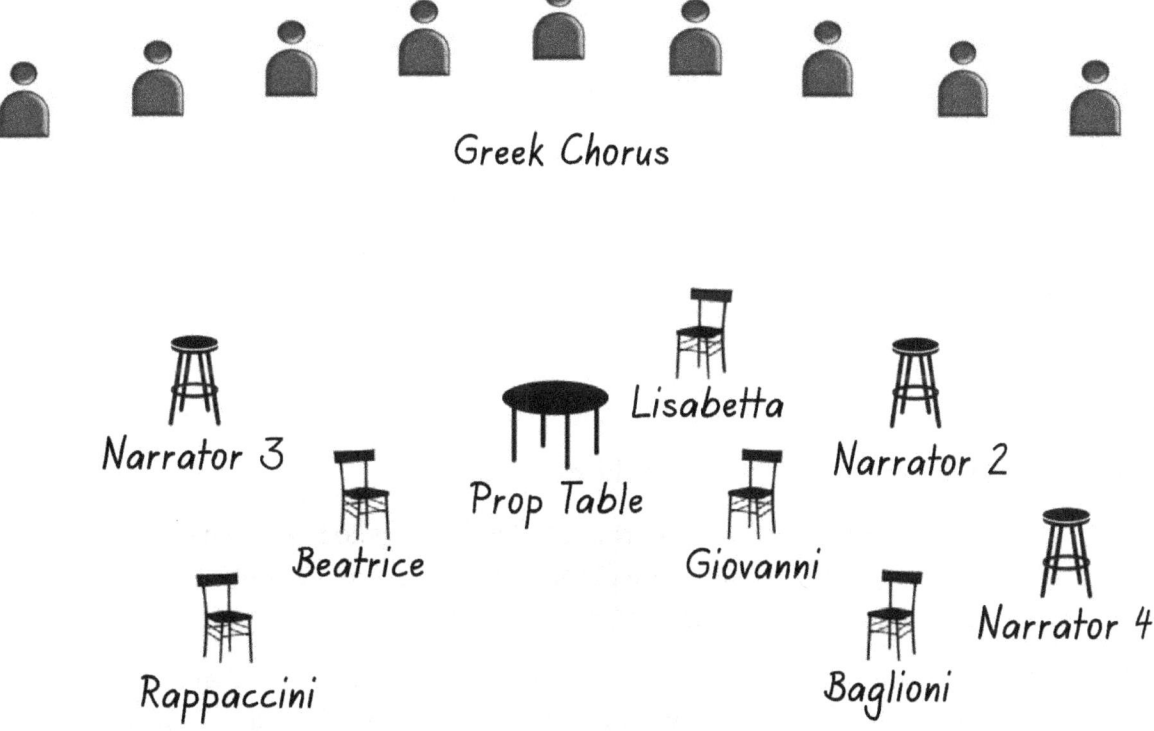

Narrator 1

Narrators are perched on tall stools, characters are seated in chairs, and the Greek chorus stands in a semicircle. This arrangement adds visual interest and role separation through three height levels.

Audience

Scene 1

NARRATOR ONE: A long time ago in Italy, a young man named Giovanni Guasconti went to study at the University of Padua. Giovanni did not have much money. He could only afford to rent one room in an old house. In the past, the house had been the palace of a nobleman who had met a tragic fate.

GREEK CHORUS: A tragic fate, a tragic fate.

NARRATOR ONE: So Giovanni had a strange sense of worry.

GREEK CHORUS: Fate, fate, fate.

LISABETTA: Signor, why do you look sad? Do you find this old house gloomy? Look out the window and you will see sunshine.

NARRATOR TWO: Giovanni looked out the window. He saw a beautiful garden with plants that had been grown with great care.

GIOVANNI: Does this garden belong to the owner of the house?

LISABETTA: Heaven forbid, signor! No, that garden belongs to Signor Giacomo Rappaccini, the famous doctor. They say he makes the plants into strong medicines. You might sometimes see the Signor Doctor and maybe even his daughter working in the garden.

NARRATOR TWO: In the center of the garden was an old fountain. All around it grew plants with gigantic leaves, and some with magnificent flowers. One shrub stood out from the others, with its splendid purple blossoms.

Giovanni saw a tall, sickly looking man working in the garden. He had gray hair, a thin gray beard, and an unfriendly face. He did not touch or smell the plants. He wore thick gloves. When he came to the purple shrub, he placed a mask over his nose and mouth. He stepped back suddenly, took off the mask, and called loudly.

RAPPACCINI: Beatrice! Beatrice!

BEATRICE: Here I am, father!

NARRATOR THREE: It was a youthful voice, musical and filled with perfume.

GREEK CHORUS: Perfume, aaaaahh, perfume.

RAPPACCINI: Beatrice, I need your help.

NARRATOR THREE: A beautiful young girl came down the garden path, breathing in the perfume of the plants.

GREEK CHORUS: Perfume, aaaaahh, perfume.

RAPPACCINI: Beatrice, our splendid treasure needs attention. But it might harm me, so from now on you must be the only one to care for it.

BEATRICE: I will care for it with pleasure.

NARRATOR THREE: She bent towards the purple shrub and opened her arms as if to embrace it.

BEATRICE: Yes, my sister, I shall care for you, and you shall reward me with your perfume breath, which to me is the breath of life!

NARRATOR ONE: It seemed to Giovanni that, instead of a girl caring for her favorite flower, she was one sister caring for another. That night Giovanni dreamed of a splendid flower and a beautiful girl. Flower and girl were different and yet the same. Both were full of some strange danger.

Scene 2

NARRATOR ONE: When Giovanni awoke, he opened the window and looked down into the garden that his dreams had made so full of mystery. He was surprised that it now looked so ordinary.

NARRATOR FOUR: That day he went to visit Signor Pietro Baglioni, a well-known Professor of Medicine at the university and a friend of Giovanni's father. Giovanni mentioned Doctor Rappaccini.

BAGLIONI: He is a greatly skilled doctor. But there are serious problems with his professional character.

GIOVANNI: And what are they?

BAGLIONI: Are you ill? Is that why you are so curious about doctors?

NARRATOR FOUR: Baglioni smiled, as if he knew Giovanni's secret.

BAGLIONI: Rappaccini cares more for science than for mankind. He uses his patients in his experiments. He would sacrifice human life, even his own life or the life of someone he loves, to gain scientific knowledge.

GIOVANNI: He must be an awful man. And yet, esteemed professor, isn't it noble to have such a strong love of science?

BAGLIONI: God forbid! His theory is that all good medicine comes from vegetable poisons. They say he has created new kinds of poison, more horrible than those in nature.

GREEK CHORUS [softly]: How much should one love science? How much should one love science?

BAGLIONI: Once in a while he has come up with what seems like a marvelous cure. But, in my opinion, he should not receive credit for such successes—they are probably just good luck—and he should be held responsible for his failures.

GREEK CHORUS [louder]: How much should one love science? How much should one love science?

GIOVANNI: Surely there is something more dear to him than science. He has a daughter.

BAGLIONI: Aha! So that is your secret!

NARRATOR FOUR: Baglioni laughed and then continued.

BAGLIONI: All the young men in Padua are wild about Signora Beatrice, but not many have seen her. I don't know much about her, but they say Rappaccini has taught her his science, and she is already qualified to be a professor. But now, Signor Giovanni, let's drink!

NARRATOR ONE: Giovanni returned to his room thinking of Rappaccini and the beautiful Beatrice. On his way home he stopped and bought a fresh bouquet of flowers. *[Lisabetta takes the bouquet of flowers from the prop table, and gives it to Giovanni. He keeps the bouquet in his hands until the next scene, when he throws it to Beatrice.]*

Scene 3

NARRATOR ONE: When Giovanni returned home, he sat where he could look down into the garden without being seen. Soon Beatrice appeared, even more beautiful than before. She had dressed in purple to look like the shrub.

NARRATOR THREE: Beatrice opened her arms, as if embracing the shrub.

BEATRICE: Give me your breath, my sister, for I am sick from breathing the common air! And give me this flower of yours.

NARRATOR THREE: Beatrice plucked one of the largest blossoms from the shrub and tucked it into her hair. *[Beatrice takes a purple flower from the prop table and puts it in her hair.]* Just then, a small lizard crawled along the path where Beatrice stood. A drop of moisture from the broken flower stem fell on the lizard's head. The lizard began to shake, then rolled over and died. Beatrice crossed herself sadly, but kept the fatal flower. Giovanni trembled.

GIOVANNI: Am I awake? Have I lost my mind? Is Beatrice beautiful? Or terrible?

GREEK CHORUS: Beautiful or terrible? Terrible or beautiful?

NARRATOR THREE: A butterfly fluttered above her head. Beatrice looked up and it fell at her feet, dead. Did it die from her breath? Again she crossed herself sadly.

GREEK CHORUS: Terrible or beautiful? Beautiful or terrible?

NARRATOR THREE: Beatrice heard a sound in Giovanni's room and looked up. Without thinking, Giovanni threw down the bouquet which he had been holding in his hand. *[Giovanni throws the bouquet of flowers to Beatrice's feet.]*

GIOVANNI: Signora, accept these flowers from Giovanni Guasconti!

BEATRICE *[picks up the bouquet]:* Thank you, signor, I accept your gift. I would like to return the favor with this precious purple flower, but if I toss it into the air, it will not reach you. So, Signor Guasconti, you must be happy with only my thanks.

NARRATOR ONE: She picked up the bouquet and ran quickly out of the garden. It seemed to Giovanni that his beautiful bouquet was beginning to wither in her hand.

[During the scene break she returns the bouquet to the prop table.]

Scene 4

NARRATOR ONE: For many days Giovanni stayed away from the window above Doctor Rappaccini's garden. Sometimes he tried to forget what he had seen by taking fast walks through the streets of Padua. But one day someone grabbed him by the arm.

BAGLIONI *[grabs Giovanni's arm]:* Signor Giovanni! Have you forgotten me?

NARRATOR FOUR: It was Baglioni, whom Giovanni had avoided. He was afraid the professor would want to know his secret.

GIOVANNI *[shakes himself free of Baglioni's grasp]:* Yes, I am Giovanni Guasconti. And you are Professor Pietro Baglioni. Now let me pass!

BAGLIONI: Not yet, not yet, Signor Giovanni Guasconti. Stand still. We need to talk.

GIOVANNI: Quickly, then, esteemed professor, quickly! Don't you see that I am in a hurry?

NARRATOR TWO: While he was speaking, a sickly old man slowly walked by, staring at Giovanni.

GREEK CHORUS: Giovanni, beware! Giovanni, beware!

BAGLIONI: It is Doctor Rappaccini! Has he ever seen you before?

GIOVANNI: Not that I know of.

GREEK CHORUS: Beware, beware, beware!

BAGLIONI: He has seen you! He is making a study of you. I know that look of his! It is the same look that he has when he bends over a bird, a mouse, or a butterfly, which he has killed with the perfume of a flower. Signor Giovanni, you have become one of Rappaccini's experiments!

GIOVANNI: Are you trying to make a fool of me? Is *that,* Signor Professor, *your* experiment?

BAGLIONI: Poor Giovanni! Rappaccini has a scientific interest in you. What part does the Signora Beatrice play in this mystery?

NARRATOR TWO: But Giovanni broke away and was gone.

GREEK CHORUS: Beware!

BAGLIONI: This must not happen. Rappaccini shall not use him for a horrible experiment.

NARRATOR ONE: Baglioni looked off in the direction where Giovanni had disappeared, and shook his head. *[Baglioni shakes his head.]*

[Use essential oil spray lightly during the scene break.]

Scene 5

NARRATOR ONE: When Giovanni arrived home, he was met by old Lisabetta, who tried to get his attention.

LISABETTA *{grasps Giovanni's arm]*: Signor, signor! Listen, signor! There is a secret entrance into the garden!

GIOVANNI: A secret entrance into Doctor Rappaccini's garden?

LISABETTA: Hush! Hush, not so loud! Yes, into the doctor's garden, where you can see all his fine plants. Many young men would give gold to go there.

GIOVANNI: Show me the way. *[He places a coin in Lisabetta's hand. She closes her hand around it and places it in her apron pocket.]*

NARRATOR TWO: Lisabetta led him to a door, which she unlocked and opened. *[Lisabetta takes a key out of her apron pocket and mimes unlocking and opening a door. Then she puts the key back into her pocket.]* Giovanni went into the garden. While he was looking at the plants, he turned and saw Beatrice. There was surprise in her face, but also pleasure.

BEATRICE: Are you are a connoisseur of flowers, signor? Did you want to see my father's rare collection? If he were here, he could tell you many strange and interesting things about these plants.

GIOVANNI: I have heard you are also very skilled in this work.

BEATRICE: Are there really such silly rumors? I have grown up with these flowers, but all I know about them is their colors and perfumes. Sometimes I wish I didn't even know that. Signor, do not believe these stories about me. Believe only what you see with your own eyes.

NARRATOR THREE: Beatrice was happy to spend time talking to Giovanni. Her experience of life had been limited to this garden, so she asked many questions about the outside world. As she spoke, there was a delightful fragrance in the air around her.

When they came to the shrub with splendid purple blossoms, Giovanni recognized its fragrance as the same as Beatrice's breath, only more powerful.

GREEK CHORUS: Beautiful or terrible? Terrible or beautiful?

NARRATOR THREE: Beatrice spoke to the shrub as if it was human.

BEATRICE: For the first time in my life, I have forgotten you!

GIOVANNI: Signora, you once promised to reward me for the bouquet I gave you, with one of these blossoms. Please let me take one.

NARRATOR THREE: He stepped towards the shrub, with his hand out to pluck a flower. But Beatrice ran forward and caught his hand to stop him. *[Giovanni mimes reaching for a flower and Beatrice stops him with her hand.]*

BEATRICE: Don't touch it! It is fatal!

GREEK CHORUS: Beautiful or terrible? Terrible or beautiful?

NARRATOR ONE: Then she ran away from him and disappeared. Giovanni saw Doctor Rappaccini watching them from the shadows. *[Doctor Rappaccini smiles slyly.]*

Scene 6

NARRATOR ONE: Giovanni awoke the next morning to a burning pain in the hand that Beatrice had touched. His hand now had a purple print of four small fingers, and his wrist had a purple print of a thumb. But Giovanni was so love-struck that he wrapped a handkerchief around his hand and wondered what had stung him. Soon he forgot his pain while thinking about Beatrice.

GREEK CHORUS: Love, aaaaahh, love!

NARRATOR TWO: After the first meeting with Beatrice, there was a second, a third, and a fourth, until meeting Beatrice in the garden was what he lived for. Beatrice felt the same way about Giovanni. And yet they had not kissed, nor held hands, nor even touched but once.

GREEK CHORUS: Love, aaaaahh, love!

NARRATOR FOUR: One morning Giovanni had an unexpected visit from Professor Baglioni.

BAGLIONI: I have been reading an old fable about an Indian prince who sent a beautiful woman with perfumed breath to Alexander the Great. Alexander fell in love with her at first sight. Then a doctor discovered her terrible secret.

GIOVANNI: And what was that?

BAGLIONI: She had been nourished with poisons from birth, until her whole body was so full of them that she also became poisonous. With the perfume of her breath, she even poisoned the air. Her love would have been poison, her embrace death! Isn't this a marvelous tale?

GIOVANNI: A childish fable. I am surprised you find time to read such nonsense.

GREEK CHORUS: Is it a fable? Or is it science? Is it imagined? Or is it real?

BAGLIONI: What fragrance is this in your apartment? It is delicious, but I do not like it. If I were to breathe it for long, I think it would make me sick. It is like the breath of a flower. Yet I see no flowers here.

GIOVANNI: There are not any flowers here. And there is not any fragrance, except in your imagination.

GREEK CHORUS: Perfume, aaaaahh, perfume.

BAGLIONI: It is not my imagination. But Rappaccini, I have heard, uses such perfumes in his medicines. The Signora Beatrice would use them, too. But beware if you drink them!

GIOVANNI: Signor, you do not know the Signora Beatrice. So you cannot understand how wrong you are about her character.

BAGLIONI: Giovanni, my poor Giovanni! Now you shall hear the truth about the poisoner Rappaccini and his poisonous daughter. Yes, she is as poisonous as she is beautiful! That old fable of the Indian woman is now true.

NARRATOR TWO: Giovanni groaned and hid his face.

BAGLIONI: Her father sacrificed his own child in his insane love of science. What will your fate be now, Giovanni? Beyond a doubt, you are chosen for some new experiment. Perhaps the result will be death, perhaps a fate more awful still!

GREEK CHORUS: A tragic fate, a tragic fate.

GIOVANNI: It is a dream, surely it is a dream!

GREEK CHORUS: Fate, fate, fate.

BAGLIONI: Do not fear. It is not too late to save yourself and maybe save Beatrice as well. Look at this vial *[He takes a vial out of his lab coat pocket and holds it up for Giovanni to see.]* One little sip of this antidote will make the most deadly poison useless. Let your Beatrice drink this, and maybe we can stop Rappaccini yet! *[He places the vial on the prop table.]*

NARRATOR ONE: And with that, Baglioni left the room.

[Use essential oil spray in a stronger intensity during the scene break.]

Scene 7

NARRATOR ONE: Giovanni decided to create a test that would show if Beatrice was really poisonous. If he could see, up close, one healthy flower dying in her hand, he would know the truth. So he bought a freshly cut bouquet of flowers. *[Lisabetta takes a bouquet of flowers from the prop table and gives it to Giovanni.]*

GREEK CHORUS: Perfume, aaaaahh, perfume.

NARRATOR TWO: But by the time he got home, the flowers were beginning to droop. Could there be poison in his breath? He saw a spider on his window. Giovanni breathed on it and the spider died.

GIOVANNI: Cursed! I am cursed!

GREEK CHORUS: Poisoned, you are poisoned!

NARRATOR THREE: At that moment he heard a sweet voice in the garden.

BEATRICE: Giovanni! Giovanni! Why are you so slow? Come down!

NARRATOR TWO: Giovanni rushed down. He had been full of anger and despair, but seeing Beatrice brought tender feelings.

GREEK CHORUS: Love, aaaaahh, love!

NARRATOR THREE: Beatrice sensed that something was wrong. They walked on together, sad and silent, until they came to the shrub with the purple blossoms. Giovanni was frightened by the enjoyment he had from their perfume.

GIOVANNI: Beatrice, where did this plant come from?

BEATRICE: My father created it.

GIOVANNI: Created it! Created it! What do you mean, Beatrice?

BEATRICE: At the hour of my birth, this plant grew from the soil, the result of his scientific work.

GREEK CHORUS: Beware, beware!

BEATRICE: Do not go near it! It could harm you. But I grew up with the plant and was nourished by its breath. I loved it as my sister. Have you suspected it? For me it was an awful doom. My father's fatal love of science has separated me from the rest of the world. Until Heaven sent you, dearest Giovanni, I was so lonely!

NARRATOR TWO: Giovanni now spoke with rage.

GIOVANNI: Cursed one! And finding your loneliness unbearable, you have tempted me into your world of horror!

BEATRICE: Giovanni!

GIOVANNI: Yes, poisonous thing! You have done it! You have made me as poisonous as you are. Now we can kiss each other and die!

BEATRICE: Giovanni, why do you say those terrible things to me? It is true that I am the horrible thing you say I am. But all you have to do is leave this garden and forget that there ever was a monster named Beatrice!

GIOVANNI: Are you pretending to be ignorant? Look at the power you have given me!

NARRATOR TWO: A swarm of insects flew above Giovanni's head. He breathed up at them, and they fell down dead.

GREEK CHORUS: Poison! Poison!

BEATRICE: I see it! It is my father's fatal science! Giovanni, it was not me! I only wanted to love you and be with you for a little time, and then to let you leave me, leaving only your memory in my heart. For, Giovanni, although my body is nourished with poison, my spirit needs love. Yes, kill me! Oh, what is death, after what you have said to me?

NARRATOR TWO: Giovanni listened to her and changed his mind.

GREEK CHORUS: Love, aaaaahh, love!

GIOVANNI: Dearest Beatrice, all is not lost. Look! *[Giovanni takes the vial from the prop table and holds it up.]* Here is a medicine that will cure us. Let us drink it together.

GREEK CHORUS: Don't drink it! Don't drink it!

BEATRICE: Give it to me! *[Beatrice grabs the vial from Giovanni.]* I will drink it first. Wait to see what happens to me before you drink it.

GREEK CHORUS *[louder, more insistent]*: Don't drink it! Don't drink it!

[Beatrice mimes drinking from the vial. Then she places it on the prop table.]

NARRATOR THREE: Rappaccini emerged from the house with a triumphant look and walked slowly towards them.

RAPPACCINI: My daughter, you are no longer alone in the world! Pluck one of these precious blossoms from your sister shrub and give it to your bridegroom. It will not harm him now! You can now live in the world beloved to one another and dreadful to all others!

GREEK CHORUS: Beloved and dreadful, dreadful, dreadful!

NARRATOR THREE: Beatrice became weaker and weaker.

BEATRICE *[puts her hand over her heart]*: Father, why did you doom my life to this misery?

GREEK CHORUS: Doom and misery, misery, misery!

RAPPACCINI: Misery! What do you mean, you foolish girl? Do you think you are doomed to have gifts against which no enemy could triumph? Do you think it is misery to be able to defeat the mightiest person with a single breath, to be as terrible as you are beautiful?

GREEK CHORUS: Beautiful or terrible? Terrible or beautiful?

RAPPACCINI: Would you rather be a weak woman, exposed to all evil and capable of none?

BEATRICE: I would rather have been loved, not feared. But now it does not matter. The perfume of these flowers will no longer poison my breath. Farewell, Giovanni! Your words of hatred are as heavy as lead within my heart. Oh, was there not more poison in your nature than in mine?

GREEK CHORUS: Who really is the poisonous one? Who really is the poisonous one?

NARRATOR THREE: Beatrice sank to the ground. Her life had been poison, and the only possible cure was death. She died there, at the feet of her father and Giovanni.

GREEK CHORUS: Who really is the poisonous one?

NARRATOR ONE: Just at that moment, Baglioni looked out from the window and called out loudly, in a tone of triumph mixed with horror.

BAGLIONI: Rappaccini! Rappaccini! And is *this* the result of your experiment?

GREEK CHORUS: How much should one love science? How much should one love science? *[Gradually fade out.]* Science, science, science, science, science, science ...

THE END

Theater Script, Secondary Level

Theater Adaptation of
Hawthorne's "Rappaccini's Daughter"
By Sharon Adelman Reyes

Characters
Doctor Giacomo Rappaccini, a scientist specializing in botany
Beatrice Rappaccini, his daughter
Lisabetta, a housekeeper
Giovanni Guasconti, a student
Professor Pietro Baglioni, of the University of Padua
Narrator

Pronunciation Key
Doctor Giacomo Rappaccini: JAHK uh mo rahp uh CHEE nee
Giovanni Guasconti: joh VAH nee gwa SKOHN tee
Beatrice Rappaccini: bay ah TREE chay rahp uh CHEE nee
Professor Pietro Baglioni: PYET ro bal YOH nee
Lisabetta: leez uh BET uh
Padua: PAH dwah
Signor: see NYOR
Signora: see NYOR uh

Tech Crew
Lights: Dim at beginning and end of production and between scenes
Music: Play at beginning and end of production and between scenes
Projection: Use PowerPoint slides as backdrops for each scene
Aroma: Spray essential oil formula into the air before Scenes 5 & 7
Ushers: As needed

Props and Costume Pieces
Doctor Giacomo Rappaccini: Laboratory jacket, gloves, face mask
Beatrice Rappaccini: Purple dress, purple flower that can be quickly attached to hair, other floral adornments
Lisabetta: Plain and dull-colored dress, apron with large skeleton key inside the pocket

Giovanni Guasconti: Textbooks, large coin in pocket, two bouquets of flowers (one wilted), wine glass, handkerchief
Professor Pietro Baglioni: Laboratory jacket with small vial inside the pocket, wine glass
Narrator: Dressed simply in a solid color
Tech Crew: Dressed in dark colors of similar style
Ushers: Dressed in similar colors

Staging

A symbolic floral barrier runs vertically through up-center stage. The down-stage area is clear. Up-right is a garden extending to the floral barrier. Plants with gigantic leaves, some with magnificent flowers, grow around an elegant fountain. One shrub has especially beautiful and profuse purple blossoms. The Narrator is seated on an elevated chair or stool at the down-right corner, separated from the action and facing the audience on an angle.

Evocative music is played and the lights are dimmed to blackness at the beginning and end of the production and during scene breaks. An aroma blend is sprayed during the breaks before Scenes 5 and 7. If desired, spray may also be used lightly before Scene 6.

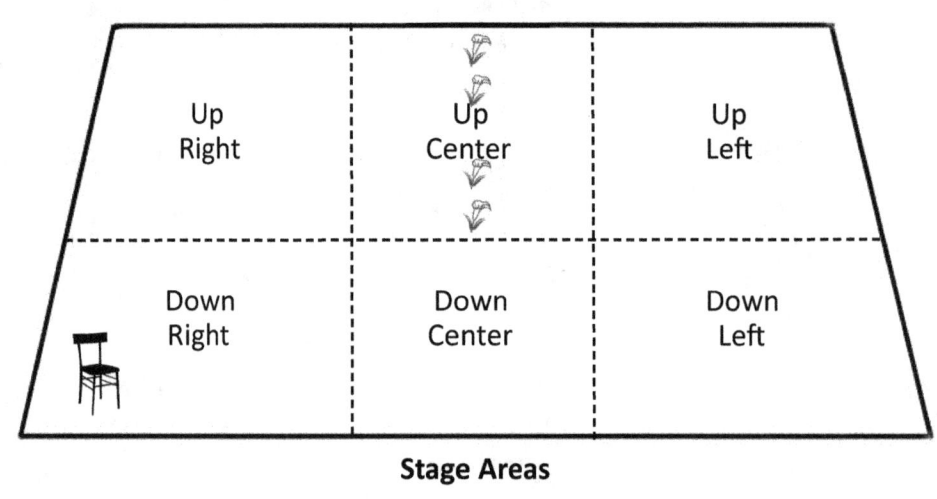

Stage Areas

Scene 1

[As the scene opens, Giovanni and Lisabetta are standing motionless up-left until their lines begin.]

NARRATOR *[to audience]:* A long time ago, a young man named Giovanni Guasconti came from Naples, in the south of Italy, to study at the University of Padua. Giovanni did not have much money. He could only afford to rent one room in an old house. In the past, the house had been the palace of a nobleman. This nobleman had met a tragic fate. And that gave Giovanni a strange sense of worry.

LISABETTA: Signor, why do you look sad? Do you find this old mansion gloomy? Put your head out of the window, and you will see sunshine as bright as the sunshine you left behind in Naples. Look at the garden beneath your window. Do you see the wondrous plants? They have been cultivated with great care.

GIOVANNI *[gazing into the garden]:* Does this garden belong to the owner of the house?

LISABETTA: Heaven forbid, signor! No, that garden is cultivated by Signor Giacomo Rappaccini, the famous doctor. It is said that he makes these plants into strong medicines. You might sometimes see the Signor Doctor and maybe even his daughter at work, gathering the strange flowers that grow in the garden. *[She exits up-left; Giovanni watches the ensuing action.]*

RAPPACCINI *[enters up-right, wearing gloves and carrying a mask. He is careful not to touch the plants or inhale their aromas, walking as if among evil spirits. He stops in front of the purple shrub, places the mask over his nose and mouth, visually examines it, then steps back, removes the mask, and calls loudly]:* Beatrice! Beatrice!

BEATRICE *[sweetly, from off-stage]:* Here I am, father! Are you in the garden?

RAPPACCINI: Yes, Beatrice, and I need your help. *[Beatrice enters from up-right, stopping to inhale the aromas of several of the plants as she moves toward him.]* Beatrice, our splendid treasure needs attention. But it might harm me, so from now on you must be the only one to care for it.

BEATRICE: I will do so gladly. *[She bends towards the shrub with purple blossoms and opens her arms as if to embrace it.]* Yes, my sister, it shall be my job to serve you, and you shall reward me with your perfume breath, which to me is the breath of life! *[She gently pats some leaves into place around the blossoms.]*

NARRATOR *[to audience]:* It seemed to Giovanni that, instead of a girl tending her favorite flower, she was one sister caring for another. But soon Doctor Rappaccini signaled to his daughter and together they left the garden. *[Rappaccini and Beatrice exit together up-right without touching.]* That night Giovanni dreamed of a splendid flower and a beautiful girl. Flower and girl were different and yet the same. Both were full of some strange danger.

[During the scene break, two chairs are placed down-center, angled toward each other and facing the audience. Baglioni and Giovanni are seated and remain motionless, each with a wine glass in hand, until their lines begin.]

Scene 2

NARRATOR *[to audience]:* When Giovanni awoke, he opened the window and gazed down into the garden that his dreams had made so full of mystery. He was surprised, and a little ashamed, to find how ordinary it appeared. That day he went to visit Signor Pietro Baglioni, a well-known Professor of Medicine at the university, to whom Giovanni had brought a letter of introduction. The professor was a kind, elderly man. He invited Giovanni to stay for dinner. Giovanni, assuming that men of science who lived in the same city must know each other, mentioned the name of Doctor Rappaccini.

BAGLIONI: He is a greatly skilled doctor. But there are serious problems with his professional character.

GIOVANNI: And what are they?

BAGLIONI: Are you ill? Is that why you are so curious about doctors? *[Smiling, as if he knows Giovanni's secret.]* But, as for Rappaccini, he cares much more for science than for mankind. His patients are interesting to him only as subjects for some new experiment. He would sacrifice human life, even his own, or whoever else was dearest to him, for the sake of adding so much as a tiny seed to the great heap of his knowledge.

GIOVANNI: He must be an awful man, indeed. And yet, esteemed professor, isn't it noble to have such a strong love of science?

BAGLIONI: God forbid! His theory is that all good medicine comes from substances that we call vegetable poisons. These he cultivates with his own hands, and is said to have produced new varieties of poison, more horrible than those occurring in nature.

It is true that now and then he has come up with what seems like a marvelous cure. But, in my opinion, he should receive little credit for such successes—they are probably just good luck—and he should be held responsible for his failures.

GIOVANNI: I don't know how much Doctor Rappaccini loves science, but surely there is something more dear to him. He has a daughter.

BAGLIONI: Aha! So now our friend Giovanni's secret is out! *[Laughs.]*

You have heard of this daughter, whom all the young men in Padua are wild about, though not many have seen her. I know little of the Signora Beatrice, except that Rappaccini is said to have instructed her deeply in his science and that, young and beautiful as she is, she is already qualified to be a professor.

But now, Signor Giovanni, let's drink! *[He holds up his wine glass in a toast.]*

[During the scene break, Baglioni and Giovanni exit with wine glasses and the chairs are removed.]

Scene 3

NARRATOR *[to audience]:* Giovanni felt a vague sense of worry as he set out for home. When he passed a florist, on an impulse he bought a fresh bouquet of flowers for Beatrice. *[Giovanni returns up-left, holding a bouquet, and peers into the garden.]* When he arrived home, he stood where he could look down into the garden without being seen. Soon, as Giovanni had half-hoped, half-feared, Beatrice appeared. She seemed even more beautiful than Giovanni had remembered. Her face had an expression of simplicity and sweetness.

BEATRICE *[enters up-right, decorated to ressemble the purple shrub, which she approaches, then opens her arms and draws it into an intimate embrace, inhaling its aroma]:* Give me your breath, my sister, for I am ill from breathing the common air! And give me this flower of yours. *[Plucks a blossom and tucks it into her hair.]*

NARRATOR *[to audience, as Beatrice mimes the appropriate action]:* Just then, a small lizard crept along the path where Beatrice stood. A drop or two of moisture from the broken stem of the flower fell on the lizard's head. The lizard began to shake, then rolled over and died. Beatrice crossed herself sadly, but kept the fatal flower.

GIOVANNI: Am I awake? Have I lost my senses? What is this being? Beautiful? Or terrible?

NARRATOR *[to audience, as Beatrice mimes the action]:* A butterfly seemed to be attracted by Beatrice and it fluttered above her head. Beatrice looked up and it fell at her feet, dead. Did the insect die from her breath? Maybe Giovanni had imagined it. Again Beatrice crossed herself sadly. A sound from Giovanni's room caused Beatrice to look up. She saw Giovanni looking down from his window. Without thinking, Giovanni threw down the bouquet which he had been holding in his hand. *[Giovanni throws the bouquet over the floral barrier, and it lands at Beatrice's feet.]*

GIOVANNI: Signora, accept these flowers from Giovanni Guasconti!

BEATRICE: Thank you, signor, I accept your gift. I would like to return the favor with this precious purple flower, but if I toss it into the air, it will not reach you. So, Signor Guasconti, you must be happy with only my thanks. *[She picks up the bouquet and quickly exits stage right, hiding it from view.]*

NARRATOR *[to audience]:* It seemed to Giovanni that his beautiful bouquet was beginning to wither in her hand.

[During the scene break Giovanni exits up-left.]

Scene 4

NARRATOR *[to audience]:* For many days afterward, Giovanni avoided the window that looked into Doctor Rappaccini's garden, as if something horrible would happen if he looked down upon it. Sometimes he tried to forget what he had seen by taking rapid walks through the streets of Padua.

[Giovanni, carrying his textbooks under his arm, walks rapidly from down-left in the direction of down-right, looking straight ahead. Baglioni follows, trying to catch up with him.]

BAGLIONI *[grabs Giovanni's upper arm and detains him]:* Signor Giovanni! Stay, my young friend! Have you forgotten me?

GIOVANNI *[shakes himself free of Baglioni's grasp]:* Yes, I am Giovanni Guasconti. And you are Professor Pietro Baglioni. Now let me pass!

BAGLIONI: Not yet, not yet, Signor Giovanni Guasconti. Stand still. We need to talk.

GIOVANNI: Quickly, then, esteemed professor, quickly! Don't you see that I am in a hurry?

[Rappaccini walks by, from down-right heading down-left, moving behind them slowly, as if he is sick. As he passes, he looks intently at Giovanni, then exists down-left.]

BAGLIONI: It is Doctor Rappaccini! Has he ever seen your face before?

GIOVANNI: Not that I know of.

BAGLIONI: He has seen you! He must have seen you! He is making a study of you. I know that look of his! It is the same look that he has when he bends over a bird, a mouse, or a butterfly that, while conducting some experiment, he has killed by the perfume of a flower. Signor Giovanni, you are certainly the subject of one of Rappaccini's experiments!

GIOVANNI: Are you trying to make a fool of me? Is *that*, Signor Professor, *your* experiment?

BAGLIONI: Patience, patience! I tell you, my poor Giovanni, that Rappaccini has a scientific interest in you. And the Signora Beatrice? What part does she play in this mystery?

[Giovanni breaks away from Baglioni and exits quickly down-right.]

BAGLIONI: This must not be. Rappaccini shall not use him for his hellish experiments!

[Baglioni looks off in Giovanni's direction and shakes his head. During the scene break Baglioni exits down-right, Lisabetta returns up-left, and essential oil spray is used lightly.]

Scene 5

NARRATOR *[to audience, as Giovanni enters up-left]*: When Giovanni reached home he was met by old Lisabetta.

LISABETTA *[grasps Giovanni's arm with urgency]*: Signor, signor! Listen, signor! There is a secret entrance into the garden!

GIOVANNI: What did you say? A secret entrance into Doctor Rappaccini's garden?

LISABETTA: Hush! Hush, not so loud! Yes, into the doctor's garden, where you may see all his fine plants. Many young men would give gold to be admitted among those flowers.

GIOVANNI *[takes a coin from his pocket and places it in Lisabetta's hand]*: Show me the way.

[Lisabetta closes her hand around the coin and places it inside her apron pocket. She leads Giovanni to the beginning of the floral barrier, mid-center, takes a key out of her apron pocket, and mimes unlocking and opening a door. Then she puts the key back inside her pocket. Giovanni steps into the garden and gazes around in wonderment, then begins to carefully observe the plants. Lisabetta exits, up-left. Giovanni is startled by the entrance of Beatrice, up-right. She walks toward him. Rappaccini is half-hidden, at up-right corner, and surreptitiously watches as Giovanni and Beatrice interact.]

BEATRICE *[with surprise and pleasure]*: You are a connoisseur of flowers, signor. It is no wonder, therefore, that you were tempted to see my father's rare collection. If he were here, he could tell you many strange and interesting things about these plants, for he has spent a lifetime in such studies, and this garden is his world.

GIOVANNI: And yourself, lady, I have heard you are also deeply skilled in this work.

BEATRICE: Are there really such silly rumors? Do people say that I am skilled in my father's science of plants? What a joke that is! No, though I have grown up among these flowers, I know no more about them than their colors and perfumes, and sometimes I wish I didn't even know that. Signor, do not believe these stories about me. Believe nothing about me except what you see with your own eyes.

NARRATOR [*to audience, as Beatrice and Giovanni meander through the garden*]: While Beatrice spoke, there was a delightful fragrance in the air around her. She was happy to spend time with Giovanni. Evidently, her experience of life had been limited to this garden. She talked about things as simple as the daylight or summer clouds, and asked questions about the city, or Giovanni's faraway home, his friends, his mother, and his sisters.

Conversing in this way, they walked toward the splendid shrub with its purple blossoms. Giovanni recognized its fragrance as identical to Beatrice's breath, only more powerful.

BEATRICE [*speaking to the purple shrub as if it were human*]: For the first time in my life, I have forgotten you!

GIOVANNI: I remember, signora, that you once promised to reward me for the bouquet I gave you, with one of these blossoms. Permit me now to pluck one.

[*Giovanni steps towards the shrub, with his hand extended to pluck a flower. Beatrice rushes forward and catches his hand to stop him, her thumb on his wrist and her four fingers on the back of his hand.*]

BEATRICE [*exclaiming in agony*]: Don't touch it! It is fatal!

[*She runs away from him and exits up-right. Giovanni watches her go and catches the eye of Doctor Rappaccini, who then moves quickly off-stage. When the stage is dark, Giovanni exits up-left.*]

Scene 6

NARRATOR [*to audience*]: Giovanni awoke the next morning to a burning and tingling pain in his right hand. This was the same hand that Beatrice had held in her own when he was about to pluck one of the purple flowers. On the back of that hand there was a purple print of four small fingers, and on his wrist there was a purple print of a thumb. But Giovanni was so love-struck that he wrapped a handkerchief around his hand and wondered what had stung him. Soon he forgot his pain while thinking about Beatrice.

After the first meeting with Beatrice, there was a second, a third, and a fourth, until meeting Beatrice in the garden was what he lived for. Beatrice felt the same way about Giovanni. And yet they had not kissed, nor held hands, nor even touched but once.

Much time had now passed since Giovanni's last meeting with Baglioni. One morning, however, Giovanni was disagreeably surprised by a visit from the professor. [*Baglioni walks from down-right to up-left, where he is met by Giovanni, who enters up-left. Gionvanni has a handerchief wrapped around his right hand and wrist. The two remain standing as they converse.]* Baglioni chatted for a few moments about the gossip of the city and the university and then brought up another topic.

BAGLIONI: Lately I have been reading the books of a well-known author and found a story of his that interested me. It is about an Indian prince who sent a beautiful woman as a present to Alexander the Great. She was as lovely as the dawn and beautiful as the sunset, but what especially distinguished her was a rich perfume in her breath. Alexander fell in love with her at first sight. Then a doctor discovered her terrible secret.

GIOVANNI: And what was that?

BAGLIONI: That this lovely woman had been nourished with poisons from birth, until her whole body was so full of them that she herself became poisonous. With the rich perfume of her breath, she poisoned the very air. Her love would have been poison, her embrace death! Isn't this a marvelous tale?

GIOVANNI: A childish fable. I am surprised you find time to read such nonsense.

BAGLIONI: By the way, what fragrance is this in your apartment? It is faint, but delicious, and yet I do not like it. If I were to breathe it for long, I think it would make me ill. It is like the breath of a flower. Yet I see no flowers in the chamber.

GIOVANNI: Nor are there any. Nor, I think, is there any fragrance, except in your imagination.

BAGLIONI: My imagination does not often play such tricks. But Rappaccini, I have heard, uses such aromas in his medicines. Likewise, the Signora Beatrice would use the same liquids. But woe unto him that drinks them!

GIOVANNI: Signor Professor, perhaps you want to protect me. But, signor, you do not know the Signora Beatrice. So you cannot understand how wrong you are about her character.

BAGLIONI: Giovanni, my poor Giovanni! I know this horrible girl far better than you know her. Now you shall hear the truth about the poisoner Rappaccini, and his poisonous daughter. Yes, she is as poisonous as she is beautiful! That old fable of the Indian woman is now true.

[Giovanni groans and hides his face in his hands.]

BAGLIONI: Her father sacrificed his own child in his insane love of science. What will your fate be now, Giovanni? Beyond a doubt, you are selected as the material of some new experiment. Perhaps the result is to be death, perhaps a fate more awful still!

GIOVANNI: It is a dream, surely it is a dream!

BAGLIONI: But do not fear. It is not too late to save yourself. Possibly, we may even succeed in bringing back this miserable child to a normal life. Look at this vial. *[He takes a vial out of his lab coat pocket and holds it up for Giovanni to see.]* One little sip of this antidote will make the most deadly poison useless. Let your Beatrice drink this, and maybe we can stop Rappaccini yet! *[Giovanni takes the vial from Baglioni, looks at it intently, and then places it in his pocket.]*

[During the scene break Giovanni and Baglioni exit up-left. Use essential oil spray in a stronger intensity.]

Scene 7

NARRATOR *[to audience]*: Giovanni decided to create a test that would determine, once and for all, if what Baglioni had said about Beatrice was true. If he could see up close one healthy flower dying in Beatrice's hand, there would be no room for further questions. With this idea, he hurried back to the florist's shop and purchased a freshly cut bouquet of flowers. *[Giovanni enters up-left holding a wilted bouquet.]*

When it was time for his daily visit with Beatrice, he told himself that her poison had not yet entered his body. Then he noticed that the flowers he held in his hand were already beginning to droop. Horror shot through him. *[Giovanni looks at the bouquet with alarm, and then drops it on the floor, where it remains through the end of the performance.]* He remembered Baglioni's remark about the fragrance in his room. It must have been the poison in his breath! He saw a spider weaving a web across his window, leaned towards the insect, and breathed upon it. *[Giovanni mimes the action.]* The spider died.

GIOVANNI: Cursed! I am cursed!

BEATRICE *[sweetly, enters from up-right as she speaks]*: Giovanni! Giovanni! It is past the hour! Why are you so slow? Come down!

[Giovanni rushes to Beatrice through the imagined doorway, mid-center.]

NARRATOR *[to audience]*: Upon seeing Beatrice, Giovanni forgot his anger and despair, and became filled with tender emotions. But Beatrice sensed that something was wrong. *[Beatrice and Giovanni greet each other and walk through the garden, without touching.]* They walked on together, sad and silent, until they came to the shrub with the splendid, purple blossoms. Giovanni was frightened by the enjoyment he had in the fragrance of its flowers.

GIOVANNI: Beatrice, where did this plant come from?

BEATRICE: My father created it.

GIOVANNI: Created it! Created it! What do you mean, Beatrice?

BEATRICE: At the hour of my birth, this plant sprang from the soil, the result of his scientific work. Do not approach it! It could harm you. But I, dearest Giovanni, I grew up and blossomed with the plant and was nourished by its breath. It was my sister. I loved it with a human affection. Have you suspected it? For me it was an awful doom, the effect of my father's fatal love of science has isolated me from the rest of the world. Until Heaven sent you, dearest Giovanni, how lonely was your poor Beatrice!

GIOVANNI *[with rage]:* Cursed one! And finding your loneliness unbearable, you have tempted me into your world of unspeakable horror!

BEATRICE: Giovanni!

GIOVANNI: Yes, poisonous thing! You have done it! You filled my veins with poison! You have made me as deadly as you are. Now we can kiss each other and die!

BEATRICE: Giovanni, why do you say those terrible things to me? It is true that I am the horrible thing you say I am. But you! All you have to do is leave this garden and forget that there ever was a monster named Beatrice!

GIOVANNI: Do you pretend ignorance? Behold this power that I have gained from the pure daughter of Rappaccini!

NARRATOR *[to audience, as Giovanni mimes the action]:* A swarm of insects flitted through the air, and circled round Giovanni's head. He breathed up at them, and smiled bitterly at Beatrice as the insects fell down dead.

BEATRICE: I see it! I see it! It is my father's fatal science! No, no, Giovanni, it was not me! Never, never! I only wanted to love you and be with you for a little time, and then to let you leave me, leaving only your memory in my heart. For, Giovanni, although my body is nourished with poison, my spirit craves love as its daily food. It is my father who has united us in this fearful condition. Yes, kill me! Oh, what is death, after what you have said to me?

GIOVANNI *[with a change of heart]:* Dearest Beatrice, all is not lost. Look! *[He takes the vial from his pocket and holds it up.]* Here is a medicine that a wise doctor gave to me. It is made from plants that are the opposite of your father's poison. Let us drink it together and we will be cured.

BEATRICE: Give it to me! *[She snatches the vial from Giovanni.]* I will drink it first. You must wait to see what happens to me before you drink it.

[Beatrice mimes drinking from the vial. At the same moment, Rappaccini emerges from upright with a triumphant expression and comes slowly towards them. He spreads his hand out over them, as if giving a blessing.]

RAPPACCINI: My daughter, you are no longer lonely in the world! Pluck one of these precious blooms from your sister shrub and give it to your bridegroom. It will not harm him now! He now stands apart from ordinary men, as you stand apart from ordinary women. You can now live in the world beloved to one another and dreadful to all others!

BEATRICE *[becomes increasingly weak and speaks with her hand on her heart]:* Father, why did you doom my life to this misery?

RAPPACCINI: Misery! What do you mean, you foolish girl? Do you think you are doomed to have such marvelous gifts, against which no enemy could triumph? Do you think it is misery to be able to defeat the mightiest person with a single breath? Do you think it is misery to be as terrible as you are beautiful? Would you rather be a weak woman, exposed to all evil and capable of none?

BEATRICE: I would rather have been loved, not feared. But now it does not matter. I am going, father, where the evil which you have tried to make part of me will pass away like a dream. The fragrance of these poisonous flowers will no longer poison my breath. Farewell, Giovanni! Your words of hatred are as heavy as lead within my heart, but they, too, will pass. Oh, was there not, from the start, more poison in your nature than in mine?

[Beatrice sinks to the ground, and dies at the feet of her father and Giovanni.]

BAGLIONI *[emerges from up-left corner, looks at the three of them, and calls out loudly in a tone of triumph mixed with horror]:* Rappaccini! Rappaccini! And is *this* the result of your experiment?

THE END

Theater Script, Secondary Level

(Booklet format; print back-to-back, then fold in half)

RAPPACCINI: Misery! What do you mean, you foolish girl? Do you think you are doomed to have such marvelous gifts, against which no enemy could triumph? Do you think it is misery to be able to defeat the mightiest person with a single breath? Do you think it is misery to be as terrible as you are beautiful? Would you rather be a weak woman, exposed to all evil and capable of none?

BEATRICE: I would rather have been loved, not feared. But now it does not matter. I am going, father, where the evil which you have tried to make part of me will pass away like a dream. The fragrance of these poisonous flowers will no longer poison my breath. Farewell, Giovanni! Your words of hatred are as heavy as lead within my heart, but they, too, will pass. Oh, was there not, from the start, more poison in your nature than in mine?

[Beatrice sinks to the ground, and dies at the feet of her father and Giovanni.]

BAGLIONI *[emerges from up-left corner, looks at the three of them, and calls out loudly in a tone of triumph mixed with horror]:* Rappaccini! Rappaccini! And is *this* the result of your experiment?

THE END

Rappaccini's Daughter
By Nathaniel Hawthorne

Theater Adaptation
By Sharon Adelman Reyes

Copyright © 2016 by DiversityLearningK12 LLC

Story Synopsis

A young man, Giovanni Guasconti, moves to Padua to attend the university there and obtains a room overlooking Doctor Rappaccini's lush, locked garden. From this vantage point Giovanni is able to view the lovely Beatrice, who is confined within, as she tends her father's plants. He gains entrance to the garden through a housekeeper who has a key to the locked gate. There he meets and falls in love with the mysterious Beatrice.

Giovanni eventually notices Beatrice's unusual and intimate relationship with the plants in the garden. He sees fresh flowers wither and insects die when exposed to her breath. His mentor, Professor Pietro Baglioni, warns Giovanni that Rappaccini is not to be trusted. But, having fallen in love with Beatrice, Giovanni does not heed his advice.

Soon Giovanni begins to notice the consequences of his association with Beatrice. He must admit that she is poisonous and he is becoming poisonous as well. In the meantime, Baglioni gives Giovanni a vial, saying that it contains an antidote for Beatrice's poison.

Giovanni confronts Beatrice with his new knowledge of her nature, and she urges him to look past her poisonous exterior to see her pure and innocent essence. Giovanni produces the vial filled with the antidote, to share it with Beatrice, so they will be able to stay together. Beatrice grabs the vial from him, so as to check its safety by drinking it first. But, as poison has been her life, the only antidote is death. Beatrice dies in the garden, as Rappaccini looks on.

---

other and die!

BEATRICE: Giovanni, why do you say those terrible things to me? It is true that I am the horrible thing you say I am. But you! All you have to do is leave this garden and forget that there ever was a monster named Beatrice!

GIOVANNI: Do you pretend ignorance? Behold this power that I have gained from the pure daughter of Rappaccini!

NARRATOR *[to audience, as Giovanni mimes the action]:* A swarm of insects flitted through the air, and circled round Giovanni's head. He breathed up at them, and smiled bitterly at Beatrice as the insects fell down dead.

BEATRICE: I see it! I see it! It is my father's fatal science! No, no, Giovanni, it was not me! Never, never! I only wanted to love you and be with you for a little time, and then to let you leave me, leaving only your memory in my heart. For, Giovanni, although my body is nourished with poison, my spirit craves love as its daily food. It is my father who has united us in this fearful condition. Yes, kill me! Oh, what is death, after what you have said to me?

GIOVANNI *[with a change of heart]:* Dearest Beatrice, all is not lost. Look! *[He takes the vial from his pocket and holds it up.]* Here is a medicine that a wise doctor gave to me. It is made from plants that are the opposite of your father's poison. Let us drink it together and we will be cured.

BEATRICE: Give it to me! *[She snatches the vial from Giovanni.]* I will drink it first. You must wait to see what happens to me before you drink it.

[Beatrice mimes drinking from the vial. At the same moment, Rappaccini emerges from up-right with a triumphant expression and comes slowly towards them. He spreads his hand out over them, as if giving a blessing.]

RAPPACCINI: My daughter, you are no longer lonely in the world! Pluck one of these precious blooms from your sister shrub and give it to your bridegroom. It will not harm him now! He now stands apart from ordinary men, as you stand apart from ordinary women. You can now live in the world beloved to one another and dreadful to all others!

BEATRICE *[becomes increasingly weak and speaks with her hand on her heart]:* Father, why did you doom my life to this misery?

you do not know the Signora Beatrice. So you cannot understand how wrong you are about her character.

BAGLIONI: Giovanni, my poor Giovanni! I know this horrible girl far better than you know her. Now you shall hear the truth about the poisoner Rappaccini, and his poisonous daughter. Yes, she is as poisonous as she is beautiful! That old fable of the Indian woman is now true.

[*Giovanni groans and hides his face in his hands.*]

BAGLIONI: Her father sacrificed his own child in his insane love of science. What will your fate be now, Giovanni? Beyond a doubt, you are selected as the material of some new experiment. Perhaps the result is to be death, perhaps a fate more awful still!

GIOVANNI: It is a dream, surely it is a dream!

BAGLIONI: But do not fear. It is not too late to save yourself. Possibly, we may even succeed in bringing back this miserable child to a normal life. Look at this vial. [*He takes a vial out of his lab coat pocket and holds it up for Giovanni to see.*] One little sip of this antidote will make the most deadly poison useless. Let your Beatrice drink this, and maybe we can stop Rappaccini yet! [*Giovanni takes the vial from Baglioni, looks at it intently, and then places it in his pocket.*]

[*During the scene break Giovanni and Baglioni exit up-left. Use essential oil spray in a stronger intensity.*]

SCENE 7

NARRATOR [*to audience*]: Giovanni decided to create a test that would determine, once and for all, if what Baglioni had said about Beatrice was true. If he could see up close one healthy flower dying in Beatrice's hand, there would be no room for further questions. With this idea, he hurried back to the florist's shop and purchased a freshly cut bouquet of flowers. [*Giovanni enters up-left holding a wilted bouquet.*]

When it was time for his daily visit with Beatrice, he told himself that her poison had not yet entered his body. Then he noticed that the flowers he held in his hand were already beginning to droop. Horror shot through

---

two bouquets of flowers (one wilted), wine glass, handkerchief

Professor Pietro Baglioni: Laboratory jacket with small vial inside the pocket, wine glass

Narrator: Dressed simply in a solid color

Tech Crew: Dressed in dark colors of similar style

Ushers: Dressed in similar colors

Staging

A symbolic floral barrier runs vertically through up-center stage. The down-stage area is clear. Up-right is a garden extending to the floral barrier. Plants with gigantic leaves, some with magnificent flowers, grow around an elegant fountain. One shrub has especially beautiful and profuse purple blossoms. The Narrator is seated on an elevated chair or stool at the down-right corner, separated from the action and facing the audience on an angle.

Evocative music is played and the lights are dimmed to blackness at the beginning and end of the production and during scene breaks. An aroma blend is sprayed during the breaks before Scenes 5 and 7. If desired, spray may also be used lightly before Scene 6.

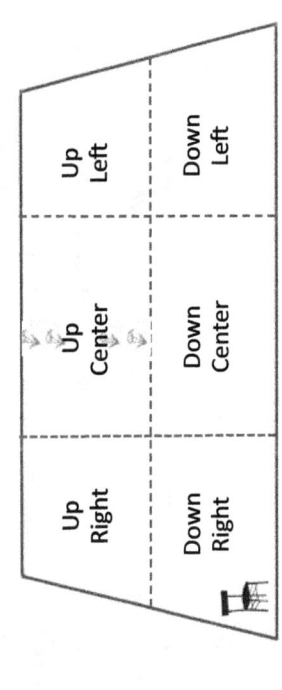

Stage Areas

Theater Adaptation of

Hawthorne's "Rappaccini's Daughter"

By Sharon Adelman Reyes

Characters

Doctor Giacomo Rappaccini, a scientist specializing in botany
Beatrice Rappaccini, his daughter
Lisabetta, a housekeeper
Giovanni Guasconti, a student
Professor Pietro Baglioni, of the University of Padua
Narrator

Pronunciation Key

Doctor Giacomo Rappaccini: JAHK uh mo rahp uh CHEE nee
Giovanni Guasconti: joh VAH nee gwa SKOHN tee
Beatrice Rappaccini: bay ah TREE chay rahp uh CHEE nee
Professor Pietro Baglioni: PYET ro bal YOH nee
Lisabetta: leez uh BET uh
Padua: PAH dwah
Signor: see NYOR
Signora: see NYOR uh

Tech Crew

Lights: Dim at beginning and end of production and between scenes
Music: Play at beginning and end of production and between scenes
Projection: Use PowerPoint slides as backdrops for each scene
Aromas: Spray essential oil formula into the air before Scenes 5 & 7
Ushers: As needed

Props and Costume Pieces

Doctor Giacomo Rappaccini: Laboratory jacket, gloves, face mask
Beatrice Rappaccini: Purple dress, purple flower that can be quickly attached to hair, other floral adornments
Lisabetta: Plain and dull-colored dress, apron with large skeleton key inside the pocket

---

him. *[Giovanni looks at the bouquet with alarm, and then drops it on the floor, where it remains through the end of the performance.]* He remembered Baglioni's remark about the fragrance in his room. It must have been the poison in his breath! He saw a spider weaving a web across his window, leaned towards the insect, and breathed upon it. *[Giovanni mimes the action.]* The spider died.

GIOVANNI: Cursed! I am cursed!

BEATRICE *[sweetly, enters from up-right as she speaks]:* Giovanni! Giovanni! It is past the hour! Why are you so slow? Come down!

[Giovanni rushes to Beatrice through the imagined doorway, mid-center.]

NARRATOR *[to audience]:* Upon seeing Beatrice, Giovanni forgot his anger and despair, and became filled with tender emotions. But Beatrice sensed that something was wrong. *[Beatrice and Giovanni greet each other and walk through the garden, without touching.]* They walked on together, sad and silent, until they came to the shrub with the splendid, purple blossoms. Giovanni was frightened by the enjoyment he had in the fragrance of its flowers.

GIOVANNI: Beatrice, where did this plant come from?

BEATRICE: My father created it.

GIOVANNI: Created it! Created it! What do you mean, Beatrice?

BEATRICE: At the hour of my birth, this plant sprang from the soil, the result of his scientific work. Do not approach it! It could harm you. But I, dearest Giovanni, I grew up and blossomed with the plant and was nourished by its breath. It was my sister. I loved it with a human affection. Have you suspected it? For me it was an awful doom, the effect of my father's fatal love of science has isolated me from the rest of the world. Until Heaven sent you, dearest Giovanni, how lonely was your poor Beatrice!

GIOVANNI *[with rage]:* Cursed one! And finding your loneliness unbearable, you have tempted me into your world of unspeakable horror!

BEATRICE: Giovanni!

GIOVANNI: Yes, poisonous thing! You have done it! You filled my veins

SCENE 1

[*As the scene opens, Giovanni and Lisabetta are standing motionless up-left until their lines begin.*]

NARRATOR [*to audience*]: A long time ago, a young man named Giovanni Guasconti came from Naples, in the south of Italy, to study at the University of Padua. Giovanni did not have much money. He could only afford to rent one room in an old house. In the past, the house had been the palace of a nobleman. This nobleman had met a tragic fate. And that gave Giovanni a strange sense of worry.

GIOVANNI [*gazing into the garden*]: Does this garden belong to the owner of the house?

LISABETTA: Signor, why do you look sad? Put your head out of the window, and you will see sunshine as bright as the sunshine you left behind in Naples. Look at the garden beneath your window. Do you see the wondrous plants? They have been cultivated with great care.

GIOVANNI: And what was that?

LISABETTA: Heaven forbid, signor! No, that garden is cultivated by Signor Giacomo Rappaccini, the famous doctor. It is said that he makes these plants into strong medicines. You might sometimes see the Signor Doctor and maybe even his daughter at work, gathering the strange flowers that grow in the garden. [*She exits up-left; Giovanni watches the ensuing action.*]

RAPPACCINI [*enters up-right, wearing gloves and carrying a mask. He is careful not to touch the plants or inhale their aromas, walking as if among evil spirits. He stops in front of the purple shrub, places the mask over his nose and mouth, visually examines it, then steps back, removes the mask, and calls loudly*]: Beatrice! Beatrice!

BEATRICE [*sweetly, from off-stage*]: Here I am, father! Are you in the garden?

RAPPACCINI: Yes, Beatrice, and I need your help. [*Beatrice enters from up-right, stopping to inhale the aromas of several of the plants as she moves toward him.*] Beatrice, our splendid treasure needs attention. But it might harm me, so from now on you must be the only one to care for it.

BEATRICE: I will do so gladly. [*She bends towards the shrub with purple*

After the first meeting with Beatrice, there was a second, a third, and a fourth, until meeting Beatrice in the garden was what he lived for. Beatrice felt the same way about Giovanni. And yet they had not kissed, nor held hands, nor even touched but once.

Much time had now passed since Giovanni's last meeting with Baglioni. One morning, however, Giovanni was disagreeably surprised by a visit from the professor. [*Baglioni walks from down-right to up-left, where he is met by Giovanni, who enters up-left. Giovanni has a handerchief wrapped around his right hand and wrist. The two remain standing as they converse.*] Baglioni chatted for a few moments about the gossip of the city and the university and then brought up another topic.

BAGLIONI: Lately I have been reading the books of a well-known author and found a story of his that interested me. It is about an Indian prince who sent a beautiful woman as a present to Alexander the Great. She was as lovely as the dawn and beautiful as the sunset, but what especially distinguished her was a rich perfume in her breath. Alexander fell in love with her at first sight. Then a doctor discovered her terrible secret.

GIOVANNI: And what was that?

BAGLIONI: That this lovely woman had been nourished with poisons from birth, until her whole body was so full of them that she herself became poisonous. With the rich perfume of her breath, she poisoned the very air. Her love would have been poison, her embrace death! Isn't this a marvelous tale?

GIOVANNI: A childish fable. I am surprised you find time to read such nonsense.

BAGLIONI: By the way, what fragrance is this in your apartment? It is faint, but delicious, and yet I do not like it. If I were to breathe it for long, I think it would make me ill. It is like the breath of a flower. Yet I see no flowers in the chamber.

GIOVANNI: Nor are there any. Nor, I think, is there any fragrance, except in your imagination.

BAGLIONI: My imagination does not often play such tricks. But Rappaccini, I have heard, uses such aromas in his medicines. Likewise, the Signora Beatrice would use the same liquids. But woe unto him that drinks them!

my job to serve you, and you shall reward me with your perfume breath, which to me is the breath of life! [*She gently pats some leaves into place around the blossoms.*]

NARRATOR [*to audience*]: It seemed to Giovanni that, instead of a girl tending her favorite flower, she was one sister caring for another. But soon Doctor Rappaccini signaled to his daughter and together they left the garden. [*Rappaccini and Beatrice exit together up-right without touching.*] That night Giovanni dreamed of a splendid flower and a beautiful girl. Flower and girl were different and yet the same. Both were full of some strange danger.

[*During the scene break, two chairs are placed down-center, angled toward each other and facing the audience. Baglioni and Giovanni are seated and remain motionless, each with a wine glass in hand, until their lines begin.*]

SCENE 2

NARRATOR [*to audience*]: When Giovanni awoke, he opened the window and gazed down into the garden that his dreams had made so full of mystery. He was surprised, and a little ashamed, to find how ordinary it appeared. That day he went to visit Signor Pietro Baglioni, a well-known Professor of Medicine at the university, to whom Giovanni had brought a letter of introduction. The professor was a kind, elderly man. He invited Giovanni to stay for dinner. Giovanni, assuming that men of science who lived in the same city must know each other, mentioned the name of Doctor Rappaccini.

BAGLIONI: He is a greatly skilled doctor. But there are serious problems with his professional character.

GIOVANNI: And what are they?

BAGLIONI: [*Smiling, as if he knows Giovanni's secret.*] But as for Rappaccini, he cares much more for science than for mankind. His patients are interesting to him only as subjects for some new experiment. He would sacrifice human life, even his own, or whoever else was dearest to him, for the sake of adding so much as a tiny seed to the great heap of his knowledge.

what you see with your own eyes.

NARRATOR [*to audience, as Beatrice and Giovanni meander through the garden*]: While Beatrice spoke, there was a delightful fragrance in the air around her. She was happy to spend time with Giovanni. Evidently, her experience of life had been limited to this garden. She talked about things as simple as the daylight or summer clouds, and asked questions about the city, or Giovanni's far-away home, his friends, his mother, and his sisters. Conversing in this way, they walked toward the splendid shrub with its purple blossoms. Giovanni recognized its fragrance as identical to Beatrice's breath, only more powerful.

BEATRICE [*speaking to the purple shrub as if it were human*]: For the first time in my life I have forgotten you!

GIOVANNI: I remember, signora, that you once promised to reward me for the bouquet I gave you, with one of these blossoms. Permit me now to pluck one.

[*Giovanni steps towards the shrub, with his hand extended to pluck a flower. Beatrice rushes forward and catches his hand to stop him, her thumb on his wrist and her four fingers on the back of his hand.*]

BEATRICE [*exclaiming in agony*]: Don't touch it! It is fatal!

[*She runs away from him, and exits up-right. Giovanni watches her go, and catches the eye of Doctor Rappaccini, who then moves quickly off-stage. When the stage is dark, Giovanni exits up-left.*]

SCENE 6

NARRATOR [*to audience*]: Giovanni awoke the next morning to a burning and tingling pain in his right hand. This was the same hand that Beatrice had held in her own when he was about to pluck one of the purple flowers. On the back of that hand there was a purple print of a thumb, and on his wrist there was a purple print of four small fingers, and struck that he wrapped a handkerchief around his hand and wondered what had stung him. Soon he forgot his pain while thinking about Beatrice.

SCENE 5

NARRATOR [to audience, as Giovanni enters up-left]: When Giovanni reached home he was met by old Lisabetta.

LISABETTA [grasps Giovanni's arm with urgency]: Signor, signor! Listen, signor! There is a secret entrance into the garden!

GIOVANNI: What did you say? A secret entrance into Doctor Rappaccini's garden?

LISABETTA: Hush! Hush, not so loud! Yes, into the doctor's garden, where you may see all his fine plants. Many young men would give gold to be admitted among those flowers.

GIOVANNI [takes a coin from his pocket and places it in Lisabetta's hand]: Show me the way.

[Lisabetta closes her hand around the coin and places it inside her apron pocket. She leads Giovanni to the beginning of the floral barrier, mid-center, takes a key out of her apron pocket, and mimes unlocking and opening a door. Then she puts the key back inside her pocket. Giovanni steps into the garden and gazes around in wonderment, then begins to carefully observe the plants. Lisabetta exits, up-left. Giovanni is startled by the entrance of Beatrice, up-right. She walks toward him. Rappaccini is half-hidden, at up-right corner, and watches surreptitiously as Giovanni and Beatrice interact.]

BEATRICE [with surprise and pleasure]: You are a connoisseur of flowers, signor. It is no wonder, therefore, that you were tempted to see my father's rare collection. If he were here, he could tell you many strange and interesting things about these plants, for he has spent a lifetime in such studies, and this garden is his world.

GIOVANNI: And yourself, lady, I have heard you are also deeply skilled in this work.

BEATRICE: Are there really such silly rumors? Do people say that I am skilled in my father's science of plants? What a joke that is! No, though I have grown up among these flowers, I know no more about them than their colors and perfumes, and sometimes I wish I didn't even know that. Signor,

---

GIOVANNI: He must be an awful man, indeed. And yet, esteemed professor, isn't it noble to have such a strong love of science?

BAGLIONI: God forbid! His theory is that all good medicine comes from substances that we call vegetable poisons. These he cultivates with his own hands, and is said to have produced new varieties of poison, more horrible than those occurring in nature.

It is true that now and then he has come up with what seems like a marvelous cure. But, in my opinion, he should receive little credit for such successes—they are probably just good luck—and he should be held responsible for his failures.

GIOVANNI: I don't know how much Doctor Rappaccini loves science, but surely there is something more dear to him. He has a daughter.

BAGLIONI: Aha! So now our friend Giovanni's secret is out! [Laughs.]

You have heard of this daughter, whom all the young men in Padua are wild about, though not many have seen her. I know little of the Signora Beatrice, except that Rappaccini is said to have instructed her deeply in his science and that, young and beautiful as she is, she is already qualified to be a professor.

But now, Signor Giovanni, let's drink! [He holds up his wine glass in a toast.]

[During the scene break, Baglioni and Giovanni exit with wine glasses and the chairs are removed.]

SCENE 3

NARRATOR [to audience]: Giovanni felt a vague sense of worry as he set out for home. When he passed a florist, on an impulse he bought a fresh bouquet of flowers for Beatrice. [Giovanni returns up-left, holding a bouquet, and peers into the garden.] When he arrived home, he stood where he could look down into the garden without being seen. Soon, as Giovanni had half-hoped, half-feared, Beatrice appeared. She seemed even more beautiful than Giovanni had remembered. Her face had an expression of simplicity and sweetness.

BEATRICE [enters up-right, decorated to resemble the purple shrub, which

inhaling its aroma]: Give me your breath, my sister, for I am ill from breathing the common air! And give me this flower of yours. [Plucks a blossom and tucks it into her hair.]

NARRATOR [to audience]: Just then, a small lizard crept along the path where Beatrice stood. A drop or two of moisture from the broken stem of the flower fell on the lizard's head. The lizard began to shake, then rolled over and died. Beatrice crossed herself sadly, but kept the fatal flower.

GIOVANNI: Am I awake? Have I lost my senses? What is this being? Beautiful? Or terrible?

NARRATOR [to audience, as Beatrice mimes the action]: A butterfly seemed to be attracted by Beatrice and it fluttered above her head. Beatrice looked up and it fell at her feet, dead. Did the insect die from her breath? Maybe Giovanni had imagined it. Again Beatrice crossed herself sadly. A sound from Giovanni's room caused Beatrice to look up. She saw Giovanni looking down from his window. Without thinking, Giovanni threw down the bouquet which he had been holding in his hand. [Giovanni throws the bouquet over the floral barrier, and it lands at Beatrice's feet.]

GIOVANNI: Signora, accept these flowers from Giovanni Guasconti!

BEATRICE: Thank you, signor, I accept your gift. I would like to return the favor with this precious purple flower, but if I toss it into the air, it will not reach you. So, Signor Guasconti, you must be happy with only my thanks. [She picks up the bouquet and quickly exits stage right, hiding it from view.]

NARRATOR [to audience]: It seemed to Giovanni that his beautiful bouquet was beginning to wither in her hand.

[During the scene break Giovanni exits up-left.]

SCENE 4

NARRATOR [to audience]: For many days afterward, Giovanni avoided the window that looked into Doctor Rappaccini's garden, as if something horrible would happen if he looked down upon it. Sometimes he tried to forget what he had seen by taking rapid walks through the streets of Padua. [Giovanni, carrying his textbooks under his arm, walks rapidly from down-

trying to catch up with him.]

BAGLIONI [grabs Giovanni's upper arm and detains him]: Signor Giovanni! Stay, my young friend! Have you forgotten me?

GIOVANNI [shakes himself free of Baglioni's grasp]: Yes, I am Giovanni Guasconti. And you are Professor Pietro Baglioni. Now let me pass!

BAGLIONI: Not yet, not yet, Signor Giovanni Guasconti. Stand still. We need to talk.

GIOVANNI: Quickly, then, esteemed professor, quickly! Don't you see that I am in a hurry?

[Rappaccini walks by, from down-right heading down-left, moving behind them slowly, as if he is sick. As he passes, he looks intently at Giovanni, then exists down-left.]

BAGLIONI: It is Doctor Rappaccini! Has he ever seen your face before?

GIOVANNI: Not that I know of.

BAGLIONI: He has seen you! He must have seen you! He is making a study of you. I know that look of his! It is the same look that he has when he bends over a bird, a mouse, or a butterfly that, while conducting some experiment, he has killed by the perfume of a flower. Signor Giovanni, you are certainly the subject of one of Rappaccini's experiments!

GIOVANNI: Are you trying to make a fool of me? Is that, Signor Professor, your experiment?

BAGLIONI: Patience, patience! I tell you, my poor Giovanni, that Rappaccini has a scientific interest in you. And the Signora Beatrice? What part does she play in this mystery?

[Giovanni breaks away from Baglioni, and exits quickly down-right.]

BAGLIONI: This must not be. Rappaccini shall not use him for his hellish experiments!

[Baglioni looks off in Giovanni's direction and shakes his head. During the scene break Baglioni exits down-right, Lisabetta returns up-left, and essential oil spray is used lightly.]

Accordion Book Template

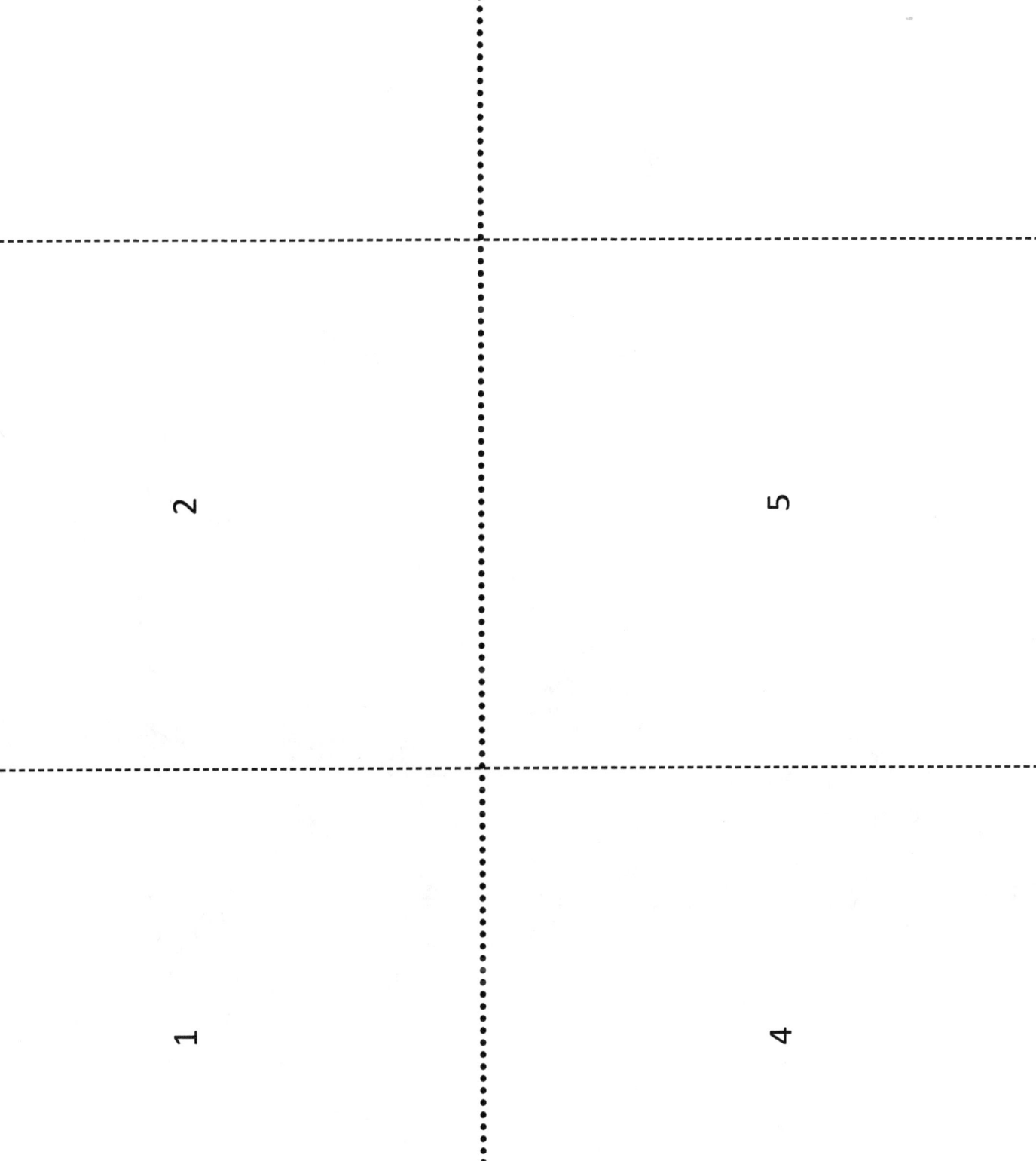

Accordion Book Template with Poetry

Poisonous Poetry
By Sharon Adelman Reyes

Flowers are growing
Lovely purple fragrant blooms
Do not believe them

Love
Falling, soaring, collapsing
Confusion

Daughter
Kind, captive
Imprisoned, sequestered, caged
Sadness, melancholy, grief, longing
Beatrice

Flowers are growing
Lovely purple fragrant blooms
Do not believe them
They beckon, they entice you
If you follow you are doomed

Antidote
warm, bright
smile, laugh, dance
remedy, cure, venom, toxicant
shiver, tremble, crush
cold, still
poison

Jazz Chant

Jazz Chant for "Rappaccini's Daughter"

(Chanted in 4/4 Rhythm)

There's a flower,

[Clap] Don't touch it!

And there's a twig,

[Clap] Don't touch it!

And there's a shrub,

[Clap] Don't touch it!

If you *[spoken in one syncopated beat]* want to live!

[Pause, clap, clap, clap]

Try writing your own Jazz Chant about "Rappaccini's Daughter"

How to Write a Rap

Parts of a Rap

- *Intro:* The section that opens the Rap and establishes its rhythm.
- *Verses:* The main parts of the Rap, which correspond to poetic stanzas.
- *Hook:* The part of the Rap that contains its themes and makes it memorable. The hook functions as a musical chorus and is often greater in musical and emotional intensity than the verses.
- *Breakdown:* A section in which the Rap is deliberately reduced to minimal elements, usually the percussion or rhythm.
- *Outro:* The ending, or passage that brings the Rap to an end, which functions as a musical coda.
- *Bridge:* An optional transition near the end of the Rap, usually occurring only once, that is musically and lyrically different from the rest of the Rap. For example, C in ABABCAB.

Structure of a Rap

The typical length of a Rap verse is 16 bars, with each bar corresponding to one sentence. Thus, a 16-bar Rap verse should have 16 sentences. The duration of a Rap is typically about four minutes and contains two or three verses. Here are some examples of Rap structure:

Three-Verse Rap

Intro — 8 bars

Verse 1 — 16 bars

Hook — 8 bars

Verse 2 — 16 bars

Hook — 8 bars

Verse 3 — 16 bars

Hook — 8 bars

Outro — 16 bars, but can be 32 bars or longer, depending on whether the rapper has something he or she would like to say by way of the outro.

Three-Verse Rap with Breakdown

Intro — 8 bars

Verse 1 — 16 bars

Hook — 8 bars

Verse 2 — 16 bars

Hook — 8 bars

Verse 3 — 16 bars

Breakdown

Hook — 8 bars

Outro — 16 bars, but can be 32 bars or longer, as needed

Two-Verse Rap

Intro — 8 bars

Verse 1 — 24 bars

Hook — 8 bars

Verse 2 — 24 bars

Hook — 8 bars

Outro — 16 bars, but can be 32 bars or longer, as needed

Simplified Rap Structure

Hook — 8 bars, or 4 bars repeated

Verse 1 — 16 bars

Hook — 8 bars, or 4 bars repeated

Verse 2 — 16 bars

Hook — 8 bars, or 4 bars repeated

Metaphor and Rhyme in Rap

Metaphor and rhyme are central features of Rap lyrics. **Metaphor** is a figure of speech that directly compares two things that are not related but have some characteristics in common. For example, the metaphor "Beatrice is a lovely flower" does not mean that Beatrice is literally a flower. Rather, it implies that she has some similar characteristics with a flower; she is sweet, beautiful, and delicate, for example. Likewise, the metaphor "Beatrice is a rattlesnake" implies that she is poisonous.

Perfect rhyme (*true/blue, mountain/fountain*) is used in Rap, but many other rhyming forms contribute to its artistry. Some of these are listed below.

Multisyllabic rhymes ("multies") are phrases in which more than one syllable rhymes. The following examples, as well as ideas for teaching multisyllabic rhymes, can be found at chasemarch.blogspot.com/2011/02/teaching-tip-multi-syllable-rhymes.html.

Multisyllabic rhymes contrasted to a normal rhyme:
- Normal rhyme — *cat/hat*
- Multi rhyme — *my cat/hi-hat*
- Longer multi rhyme — *bit my cat/hit the hi-hat*

Multisyllabic rhymes for a cold winter day:
- Old spinsters pray
- Gold winners play
- The old sinister man from the bay
- Fold printer paper this way
- Polled the Prime Minister today

Internal rhyme occurs within a line or a passage, either at random or in a pattern, for example, as in Edgar Allan Poe's poem "The Raven":

> *Once upon a midnight <u>dreary,</u> while I pondered, weak and <u>weary,</u>*
> *Over many a quaint and curious volume of forgotten lore —*
> *While I nodded, nearly <u>napping,</u> suddenly there came a <u>tapping,</u>*
> *As of someone gently <u>rapping, rapping</u> at my chamber door.*
> *"'Tis some visiter," I muttered, "<u>tapping</u> at my chamber door" —*
> *Only this and nothing more.*

Slant rhyme (a.k.a. imperfect rhyme, half rhyme, approximate rhyme, near rhyme, off rhyme, or oblique rhyme) is close but not exact, such as *dark/heart*. Here is a slant rhyme used in a poem by Emily Dickinson:

> *Hope is the thing with <u>feathers</u>*
> *That perches in the <u>soul,</u>*
> *And sings the tune without the words,*
> *And never stops at <u>all</u>.*

Identical rhyme is created by repeating a word, for example: *stone/stone*.

Rich rhyme refers to homonyms that rhyme with each other: *blue/blew, guessed/guest*.

Assonant rhyme has similar vowels and different consonants: *dip/limp, man/can't*.

Consonant rhyme has similar consonants and different vowels: *limp/lump, bit/bet*.

Macaronic rhyme uses more than one language and offers an excellent opportunity to explore bilingual poetry. Students soon discover they can create more rhymes when they have a larger supply of rhyming words to choose from. For example, *con* (English) and *pan* (Spanish).

Suggested Process for Creating a Rap

- Select a topic and a beat.
- Select a structure.
- Write the hook (chorus) containing the theme of the Rap.
- Write the verses; each verse should be 16 bars.
- Use metaphors, an effective way to convey complex concepts succinctly.
- Rap and refine. Practice rapping in the chosen beat (a metronome may be helpful). Refine the written verses. If desired, add a pause or two to emphasize an important point in the Rap.
- Memorize the Rap.
- Produce (record) or perform the Rap.

"Rappaccini's Rap"

Rappaccini's Rap
by Sharon Adelman Reyes

I've got some lovely plants, young man, I've got Beatrice, my daughter
Come down into my garden and for Beatrice you'll be water
Give her a kiss, when you leave you will miss her mysterious charm
I have raised her with love, don't worry, what's the harm? *[Repeat hook]*

I want Beatrice to marry—how far should a dad go?
If I see you breathe her essence, should I stop and tell you "No"?
I won't tell you whoa, won't let you go, won't ever say no, because I know
It's what I planned all these years, how easily, how eagerly you are lured
If I see you touch her gently, if I see you grip her hand
I will hide and slyly chuckle, "Now forever you're her man!"
So I'll lure you to my garden, let the housemaid have the key
I will tell her to entice you, that soon Beatrice you will see
No matter what they say, Beatrice will pull you back
They will tell you, "Go home, just say no, just turn your back."
But it's mysterious, so mysterious, you grow delirious, so delirious
It is la-la-la-la-la-la-love, so you are filled, so filled
It is la-la-la-la-la-la-love, so you fold, you fold
This is real, real, real, real, it is no prank
From love you reel, reel, reel, reel, you are a man
You may try to escape, but you can't, no you can't

I've got some lovely plants, young man, I've got Beatrice, my daughter
Come down into my garden and for Beatrice you'll be water
Give her a kiss, when you leave you will miss her mysterious charm
I have raised her with love, don't worry, what's the harm? *[Repeat hook]*

You have come into my garden, which for me is no surprise
When you look into her eyes, my Beatrice tells no lies
I surmise that you have found that you cannot leave, but do not grieve
For you have what all men crave, you have power and men will fear you
So enjoy this tender moment, do not fight it, hold her near you
Wait! Stop! Whoa! No! Don't drink what's in that vial!
Wait! Stop! Whoa! No! Don't drink it for its vile! It is vile!
She drank it, she is falling, she is sinking to the ground
Oh my daughter, you are my water, without you I am lost
I never once imagined love for science would have such cost
Goodbye my princess, goodbye my angel, fragrant child, ciao bella,
Oh, Giovanni, we are united in our grieving, I now tell ya
Sister flower my dear daughter, fragrant purple, silent hurtful
Lost your sister, lost my daughter, gained a son who's not compliant
So welcome to my garden, it's now yours as it was hers, catch
A bride through garden windows and I'll have grandchildren of science

I've got some lovely plants, young man, I've got Beatrice, my daughter
Come down into my garden and for Beatrice you'll be water
Give her a kiss, when you leave you will miss her mysterious charm
I have raised her with love, don't worry, what's the harm? *[Repeat hook]*

EXPLORING "RAPPACCINI'S RAP"
(Teacher Reference)

Can you find these features in "Rappaccini's Rap?
- Metaphor
- Perfect rhyme
- Multisyllabic rhyme ("multie")
- Internal rhyme
- Slant rhyme
- Identical rhyme
- Rich rhyme
- Assonant rhyme
- Consonant rhyme
- Macaronic rhyme

Now that Beatrice has died, what is Doctor Rappaccini's hope for the future? Why would he have such a hope?

Do you think there is any possibility that his hope could become a reality? Why or why not?

If it did, what could be the possible consequence(s)?

Do you think Doctor Rappaccini will reconsider his love of science? Why or why not?

Will Beatrice's death cause Doctor Rappaccini to reconsider his future actions? Why or why not?

Does he have any feelings of empathy or compassion for Beatrice or any other human being? Give evidence for your belief.

Why was the metaphor of water used in "Rappaccini's Rap?"

What rhyme forms used within the Rap were most effective for you?

"Rappaccini's Rap" Answer Key

<u>Metaphor</u>	*Identical rhyme*
PERFECT RHYME	**Rich rhyme**
Multisyllabic rhyme	Assonant rhyme
INTERNAL RHYME	Consonant rhyme
Slant rhyme	Macaronic rhyme

I've got some lovely plants, young man, I've got Beatrice, my DAUGHTER
Come down into my garden and <u>for Beatrice you'll be WATER</u>
Give her a KISS, when you leave you will MISS her mysterious CHARM
I have raised her with love, don't worry, what's the HARM?

I want Beatrice to marry—how far should a dad GO?
If I see you breathe her essence, should I stop and tell you "NO"? [also, **No**]
I won't tell you WHOA, won't let you GO, won't ever say NO, because I **know**
It's what I planned all these years, how easily, how eagerly you are lured
If I see you touch her gently, if I see you grip her `hand`
I will hide and slyly chuckle, "Now forever you're her `man`!"
So I'll lure you to my garden, let the housemaid have the KEY
I will tell her to entice you, that soon Beatrice you will SEE
No matter what they say, Beatrice will pull you *back*
They will tell you, "Go home, just say no, just turn your *back*."
But it's mysterious, **so mysterious,** you **grow delirious,** so *delirious*
It is la-la-la-la-la-la-love, so you are filled, so `filled`
It is la-la-la-la-la-la-love, so you fold, you `fold`
This is **real, real, real, real,** it is no prank [also, REAL]
From love you **reel, reel, reel, reel,** you are a `man` [also, REEL]
You may try to escape, but you can't, no you `can't`

I've got some lovely plants, young man, I've got Beatrice, my DAUGHTER
Come down into my garden and <u>for Beatrice you'll be WATER</u>
Give her a KISS, when you leave you will MISS her mysterious CHARM
I have raised her with love, don't worry, what's the HARM?

You have come into my garden, which for me is no SURPRISE
When you look into her EYES, my Beatrice tells no LIES [also, LIES]
I surmise that you have found that you cannot LEAVE, but do not GRIEVE
For you have what all men crave, you have power and men will fear *you*
So enjoy this tender moment, do not fight it, hold her near *you*
Wait! Stop! WHOA! NO! Don't drink what's in that **vial!**
Wait! Stop! WHOA! NO! Don't drink it for its **vile!** It is **vile!**
She drank it, she is falling, she is sinking to the ground
<u>Oh my daughter, you are my water</u>, without you I am LOST
I never once imagined love for science would have such COST
Goodbye my princess, goodbye my angel, fragrant child, *ciao bella*,
Oh, Giovanni, we are united in our grieving, I now *tell ya*
Sister flower my dear daughter, fragrant *purple*, silent *hurtful* [also, PURPLE, HURTFUL]
Lost your sister, lost my daughter, gained a son who's not *compliant*
So welcome to my garden, it's now yours as it was hers, catch
A bride through garden windows and I'll have grandchildren of *science*

I've got some lovely plants, young man, I've got Beatrice, my DAUGHTER
Come down into my garden and <u>for Beatrice you'll be WATER</u>
Give her a kiss, when you leave you will miss her mysterious CHARM
I have raised her with love, don't worry, what's the HARM?

Acknowledgments

This book evolved over many years. For their valuable contributions to the process I am grateful to many friends and colleagues, including:

Mary Carol Combs, of the University of Arizona College of Education, for her idea of incorporating a Greek Chorus into a scripted classroom performance.

Melissa Ketrinos, for awakening my interest in the application of aroma therapy to multiple contexts, and for contributing the information on pages 12–13.

Glenna A. Reyes, for her artwork illustrating the Character Mind Maps and Character Self-Portraits on pages 23–24.

Rob Chambers, Theatre Department Head, and Tina Boyer Brown, Creative Writing Department Head, at the Chicago High School for the Arts, who allowed me to field test a Readers Theater script with their students and offered helpful suggestions for revision.

Rob's class of sophomore musical theater majors and Tina's class of creative writing majors, which provided the insightful commentary needed to improve the Readers Theater scripts. In addition, Mariah Wolfe proposed the idea of creating and including a theater script.

Thanks to these sophomore musical theater majors:

Toney Araujo, Lish Carroll, Maggie Dabrowski, Eli Guardiola, Gilli Leonard, Joshlyn Lomax, Subi Mitchell, Jocelyn Neidballa, La'Tia Owens, Dina Pérez, Brooke Person, Alyssa Rodríguez, Rose Saunderson, Henry Schellinger, Clare Sheedy, Gabrielle Smith, Mariah Wolfe, and Kaylah Wright.

Thanks also to these freshman and sophomore creative writing majors:

Maria-Isabel Allen-Cardona, Pachaun Begley, Maya Bensett, Vincent Byas, Haley Cao, Tania Evans, Ysobel Gallo, Nathalia Harris, Calvin Holmes, Nicolas Joy, Cedric Lewis, Kathryn Malate, Faith Moreno, Valeria Pacheco, Damayanti Wallace, Oona Winners, and Paulina Zuñiga.

And thanks to the teachers who empowered them: Rob Chambers and Tina Boyer Brown.

Finally, a special thanks to James Crawford, who not only encouraged me to write this book, but single-handedly did all of the copyediting, graphic design, and book layout. Without him, this book would not have been possible.

About DiversityLearningK12

Specializing in bilingual, ESL, and multicultural education, DiversityLearningK12 is a consulting group that provides professional development, keynote presentations, program design, educational publishing, and related services. For more information, please visit us at www.diversitylearningk12.com or email us at info@diversitylearningk12.com.

Also Available from DiversityLearningK12 ...

"A must read for parents and teachers who value bilingualism, biculturalism, and positive identity construction for their children. Highly recommended."
— *Choice*

"Refreshing and inspiring ... If you are interested in learning how educators and parents can promote language acquisition, creating inventors who think creatively and (gasp!) even achieve excellent results on academic tests, this is the book for you."
— *Creative Educator*

"The beauty of *Diary of a Bilingual School* is that anyone can read this book and gain something from it. Parents of bilingual children will learn tools on how to help their children's education thrive. Bilingual educators and administrators will gain insights and tips on how to create the best bilingual classroom experience possible."
— *Multilingual Living*

Diary of a Bilingual School

Sharon Adelman Reyes & James Crawford

2012 • 136 pages • 6" x 9"
ISBN: 978-0-9847317-0-1
Paperback: $19.95 • Amazon Kindle: $4.99
Bulk orders: info@diversitylearningk12.com

DUAL IMMERSION, a popular new way to cultivate bilingualism, is capturing the attention of parents and educators alike. By bringing together children from diverse backgrounds to learn each other's languages in a natural setting, it has proved far more effective at cultivating fluency than traditional approaches.

But how do these programs actually work? What goes on in dual immersion classrooms? And what is it that makes them so effective?

Diary of a Bilingual School answers these questions with a unique mix of narratives and analysis. Depicting a year in the life of a second-grade classroom, it demonstrates what can happen when the instruction is bilingual and the curriculum is constructivist.

The book focuses on Chicago's Inter-American Magnet School, one of the nation's most acclaimed dual immersion programs, where children thrive in an environment that unlocks their intellectual curiosity and enthusiasm for learning. Simultaneously, without conscious effort, they become proficient in two languages and at home in a culture that differs from their own.

For those who want to discover the benefits of dual immersion for their children or for their students—or who want to learn more about child-centered approaches to teaching—*Diary of a Bilingual School* is a must.

DiversityLearningK12
PORTLAND, OREGON

Also Available from DiversityLearningK12 ...

© 2014 • 428 pages • 7.44" x 9.69"
ISBN: 978-0-9847317-2-5
Paperback: $29.95 • Amazon Kindle: $19.95
Bulk orders: info@diversitylearningk12.com

LANGUAGE PROFICIENCY IS MULTIDIMENSIONAL. While conversational skills are essential for social interaction, they are insufficient for most academic purposes. To be successful, teachers and students must acquire a firm and accurate command of subject-area vocabulary.

Even though a growing number of Americans speak Spanish at home, the United States has a severe shortage of professionals with fully developed academic skills in Spanish. This poses a special challenge for bilingual classrooms. Educators must be able to identify *la palabra justa* — the right word — in preparing or presenting a lesson, especially when providing content instruction and second-language input at the same time.

Recognizing an acute need, the editors of this volume brought together an international team of language teachers, teacher educators, and other bilingual professionals to create an English-Spanish / Español-Inglés glossary. **La Palabra Justa** features more than 24,000 entries covering the academic vocabulary needed in K–12 education.

Unlike a dictionary, the glossary offers a quick, user-friendly way to find translations of key terms in context. Sections include:

- **Language Arts:** *Grammar & Composition, Literature, Languages*
- **Mathematics:** *Arithmetic & Algebra, Geometry, Probability & Data Analysis, Numbers & Measures*
- **Science:** *Earth Sciences, Life Sciences, Physical Sciences, Inquiry & Process*
- **Social Studies:** *Civics & Government, Economics & Finance, Geography, History*
- **Fine Arts:** *Performing Arts, Visual Arts*
- **Technology**
- **School Life:** *Holidays & Celebrations, School Routines & Activities, Field Trips & Transportation, School Library, Playground & Sports, Student Health, Special Needs, Conduct & Discipline*

DiversityLearningK12
PORTLAND, OREGON

© 2013 • 152 pp • 8½" x 11"
Paperback: $26.95
ISBN: 978-0-9847317-3-2
Bulk orders: info@diversitylearningk12.com

Also Available from DiversityLearningK12 ...

"With **Engage the Creative Arts,** we are entering a new era in language instruction. This book vastly expands the options for providing second language students with what they really need: input that is both comprehensible and highly interesting, so interesting that students forget it is in another language. It is sure to make teaching second languages not only much more pleasant than current approaches, but also much more effective."

— *Stephen Krashen, Professor Emeritus University of Southern California*

MEETING THE NEEDS OF ENGLISH LANGUAGE LEARNERS is one of the biggest challenges facing American schools today. Practical classroom strategies are essential. But it is also critical for educators to understand the rationale behind them: why a technique or methodology is working or not working for their students. *Engage the Creative Arts* is designed to build that understanding while also stimulating teachers' imagination to help them invent new strategies of their own.

The book introduces the **ENGAGE Framework for Sheltering and Scaffolding Language the Natural Way.** It emphasizes methodologies that are grounded in a constructivist educational philosophy and a comprehensive theory of language acquisition. Rather than prescriptive, step-by-step recipes for instruction, it features strategies that are open-ended, creative, and best of all, engaging for students.

Engage the Creative Arts is full of hands-on, ready-to-use activities in dramatic arts, creative writing, music and rhythm, dance and movement, and visual arts, along with ideas for developing many more. But the ENGAGE Framework can be applied to any academic content area. And the strategies in this book are designed for all teachers who work with second language learners, whether in bilingual, English as a second language, dual immersion, heritage language, or world language classrooms.

DiversityLearningK12
PORTLAND, OREGON

Also Available from DiversityLearningK12 ...

"By far the most complete, the most thorough, and the most insightful volume ever done in the field."

— Stephen Krashen
Professor Emeritus
University of Southern California

**NEWLY UPDATED
KINDLE EDITION, 2015
NOW AVAILABLE ON AMAZON**

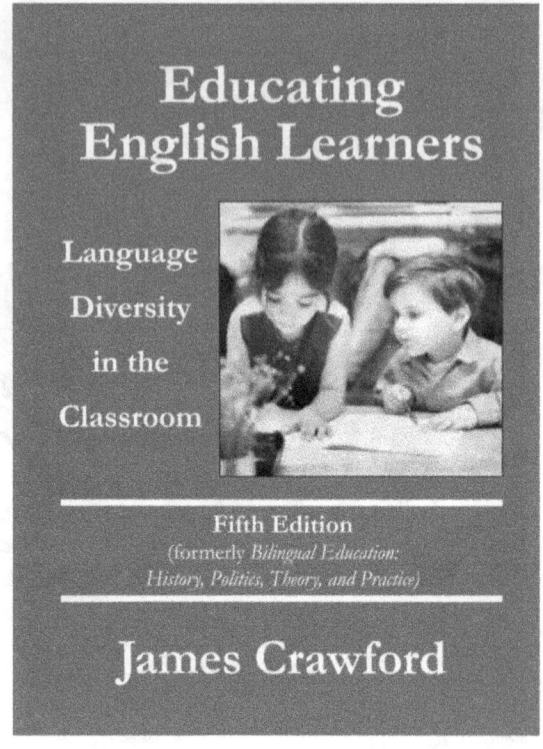

Long popular with students and professors alike, *Educating English Learners,* 5th edition (2004), differs from typical academic texts in several ways. Its journalistic style and presentation, drawn from real-world programs and events, have made it one of the most readable books used in teacher-education programs.

Author James Crawford, a former Washington Editor of *Education Week,* offers a broad perspective encompassing policy and politics as well as research and pedagogy. Avoiding the "everything but the kitchen sink" approach, he stresses in-depth discussion of key concepts and controversies that are most relevant to classroom teachers. Crawford relies not only on academic sources, but also on interviews he has conducted over many years with researchers, practitioners, policymakers, and advocates.

In addition, the new Kindle edition provides extensive links to bibliographical references, plus a Web-based Online Resource Guide featuring hundreds of primary source materials, research studies, legislation and litigation, ERIC Digests, historical documents, government reports, and other aids to further research.

DiversityLearningK12
PORTLAND, OREGON

© 2015 • 128 pp • 6" x 9"
Paperback: $17.95 • Amazon Kindle: $9.99
ISBN: 978-0-9847317-4-9
Bulk orders: info@diversitylearningk12.com

Also Available from DiversityLearningK12 …

"This slim but pithy handbook is a rich and highly accessible resource for in-service and preservice teachers, parents, administrators, and laypeople interested in issues related to English language learners."

— Holly Hansen-Thomas
TESOL's Essential Teacher

CONSIDER ANY QUESTION you may have about working with English language learners (ELLs), and it's quite likely you will find the answer in this indispensable book. Authors James Crawford and Stephen Krashen use a straightforward Q&A format to address educators' concerns in a concise and accessible way—everything from "What types of instructional programs are designed to address the needs of ELLs?" to "Do ELLs need to be taught phonics?" The book provides a state-of-the-art guide to the field, written to focus sharply on the major issues facing English language learners and the educators who work with them.

On the opening page, Crawford and Krashen state the essential aim of their book: "It's no secret that immigrants are transforming American classrooms. Or that increasing numbers of our students are ELLs … a trend that poses unique challenges and opportunities for schools. How should educators respond?"

Read to suit your own needs—straight through from first question to last, or selectively to glean expert advice on issues of special interest. Either way, you'll close English Learners in American Classrooms better equipped to make a difference for the ELLs in your classroom, school, and community.

DiversityLearningK12
PORTLAND, OREGON

www.ingramcontent.com/pod-product-compliance
Lightning Source LLC
Chambersburg PA
CBHW080245170426
43192CB00014BA/2575